BUTTERFLIES ON

The pleasures and pitfalls o

With love
Eleanor Francis
(Helen Newman)

This book is an account of actual events and experiences in the eight years since taking early retirement from the National Health Service in summer 1992, when my husband and I decided to purchase a small property in the Charente-Maritime region of south-west France. Names have been changed in order to protect the characters involved, preserve anonymity and minimise embarrassment.

Mimosa is a delicate winter-flowering shrub found in various parts of France including the Charente-Maritime. It would therefore be most unusual for its luxuriant sprays of fluffy golden blooms to entice the brightly coloured butterflies that adorn the garden during the warm summer months. When considering the purchase of a property in France however, one learns to embrace the unusual, to expect the unexpected...

Eleanor Francis, 2001

BUTTERFLIES ON MIMOSA

The pleasures and pitfalls of owning a gîte

ELEANOR FRANCIS
Illustrated by PATRICIA KELSALL

an imprint of
ANNE LOADER
PUBLICATIONS

This book is dedicated to my long-suffering husband and daughter, for their unswerving support and devotion, and to our friends, Olivia and Vic, who share our passion for France.
EF

ISBN 1 901253 23 6

First published April 2001

© Eleanor Francis
© Patricia Kelsall

Published in Gt Britain by:
Léonie Press
an imprint of
Anne Loader Publications
13 Vale Road
Hartford
Northwich
Cheshire CW8 1PL
Tel: 01606 75660   Fax: 01606 77609
E-mail: anne@leoniepress.com
Websites: http://www.aloaderpubs.co.uk
http://www.leoniepress.com
http://www.sleepydogdreams.com

ABOUT THE AUTHOR

Eleanor Francis was born and grew up in York, where she qualified as a Radiographer in 1961. Shortly afterwards she moved to London. She worked as a Radiographer and Senior Radiographer at Guys Hospital from 1963-1970, and as a Senior Radiographer, and Superintendent Radiographer specialising in angiographic and cardiovascular work, at Kings College Hospital, London, from 1970-1983. In 1975 she attained the Higher Diploma of the College of Radiographers.

She married a professional horn player, instrumental teacher and organist in April 1983 and they have one daughter.

In July of that year she was appointed Superintendent Radiographer for Bromley Hospital in Kent, and later Unit Radiography manager, Bromley and Beckenham Hospitals. Disillusioned by the various changes and reorganisations within the National Health Service, she took early retirement in 1992.

LIST OF ILLUSTRATIONS

CONTENTS

Our house as it was eventually to look

CHAPTER ONE

BIRTH OF A DREAM

The usual welcoming glow of the Charente-Maritime had unfortunately abandoned us, and the damp greyness of impending winter was undoubtedly emerging. We were now too late to pick up the keys from the *immobilier* to our newly acquired French home. We had therefore made hasty telephone arrangements to pick them up at the house of the estate agent's assistant Martine, who apparently lived in the adjoining hamlet, to which we were directed, using a combination of my limited French and *mademoiselle*'s inadequate English.

The villages, already shuttered up for the winter, with an occasional chink of light just visible, seemed bare and deserted as we hurtled through the final three kilometres of narrow country lanes. A rabbit darting across our headlights was the only apparent sign of life, and the countryside generally looked unusually impoverished, with fields of maize and sunflowers displaying merely brittle stubble. Finding Martine's house proved more difficult than we imagined. There were no names, no numbers, and instructions like "facing the stream," or "turn right by the fig tree" were considered adequate to enlighten us to the knowledge of local residents' whereabouts. At last, keys clutched firmly in hand, we rounded the final bend to take our first view of *Chez Nous.*

The house loomed suddenly before us, stark and threatening in the moonlight, not a bit as we remembered it – quaintly nestling behind an abundance of roses and softly clad in Virginia creeper. Cracks and holes that had passed unnoticed in the brilliance of the August sun were now distinctly evident. The neatly clipped roses that had adorned the front of the cottage had long since lost their startling red and pink blooms and unruly branches had forced and twisted their way to the upper floor shutters, looking unkempt and uncared for. Nettles and wild flowers had replaced the neatly trimmed grass and were sprouting freely around the side and rear of the cottage. The Virginia creeper had shed its leaves on to the patio, and these lay in huge red and brown drifts against the garden gate, barring our entrance into the garden. Along the rear house wall the line of pink Japanese anemones had shrivelled into rigid brown stems.

Determined not to allow our initial optimism to sag, we quickly without further inspection entered the building by the rear kitchen door, beside which the post-box, covered in flaking white paint, lay balanced upon a large stone. The kitchen in its present state was easily the worst room in the house. A big room, it was empty apart from a large square ancient porcelain sink, with a T-shaped, well-eroded tap that emerged from the wall above the sink and dripped constantly, an old heavy rectangular kitchen table covered in ghastly pink formica, and a solitary formica cabinet with an upper door hanging precariously from one hinge. The latter had been used by the previous owners to house every kitchen utensil they happened to possess. The room did however, have tremendous potential. An old portable cylinder-gas cooker stood in the remains of an old fireplace in one corner of the room. The kitchen had an extremely high pine-covered ceiling that sloped abruptly down to average height above the rear entrance.

A worn stone step led up from the kitchen into the living room through a low doorway. It was a bright and airy dual-aspect room, with French windows leading on to a patio and pretty garden, and ahead a triple-opening window, each window panel divided into small wooden panes, looking out across a country lane over a field to the woods beyond. This room had first attracted us to the cottage, with its beamed ceiling and large open fire-place distinguished by its beautiful polished oak mantelpiece, full eight inches thick with a characteristic but rather endearing split across one corner of it. The mottled black and white marble floor tiles, we discovered, had been wedged, rather than cemented together. We had managed to lift one of them with difficulty and discovered the tiles were a good two centimetres thick, and lay like a giant chessboard on a dusty cement base.

A room leading off the living room, to the right, had been used by the previous owners as an office, but would make a splendid bedroom, again with a triple panelled window over-looking fields and woods, and with an elegant arch at the far end of the room. These old thick stone walled houses had no foundations, and damp stains, derived from the salt and sand upon which the house stood, had appeared on the two outside walls of the room to a height of almost three feet. The room was fully carpeted in French navy, but this was badly worn and stained throughout its entirety. A pungent earthy dampness permeated the whole room, a definite deterrent to anyone wishing to linger there too long.

The *salle d'eau* was a very strange affair, opening on to the blue-carpeted room on the one side and on the other side into an integral garage. A cubicled-off toilet occupied one corner of the room. The toilet bowl was an incongruous outrage. We remembered being intrigued and mildly curious as to how it worked. There was no water tank attached to the toilet, mere-ly one narrow-gauge cold water pipe linked in at the rear. At the base of the toilet bowl was a twelve-centimetre metal lever connected to a metal ball. In order to operate this one had to be ingenious and lucky enough to engage the metal ball with a second metal ball, *et voilà*, a trap opened at the base of the toi-let, which sent approximately two teaspoons of water trickling into the bowl. We were adamant – this mediaeval monstrosity had to go! Adjoining the toilet and completing one short side of the room was a tiled shower area, with a rather corroded, primi-tive shower attachment and plain white tiles sporting multi-tudes of fine cracks with age. Immediately in front of the shower was a bidet. Occupying the bowl of the bidet was a rivulet of thick, hard brown scale. Both taps had seized up, a fact that had gone unnoticed on our initial visit. The doors situated at either side of the long walls of the room appeared to divide up the room lengthways, the opposite end being used as a laundry section, with a top-loading automatic washing machine and various laundry baskets.

Exiting the shower room on the garage side was a bit of a shock. The area was relatively undeveloped and used as a storage space for garden machinery and implements, DIY tools, paint and two bicycles that would have graced any antique shop. The Roman roof tiles were visible and even odd bits of daylight were revealed. Exposed original roof timbers, weakened by woodworm infestation, left us deliberating on the ability of the timbers to actually support the roof. On the large outer wall an upper and lower redundant window had been cemented in, reducing the natural light to the garage, and giving an unsightly appearance to the whole of the outside rear wall of the cottage. The garage door consisted of rotting timber and would require replacing; already the moth-eaten lower edge of the door beckoned the wildlife that existed in just about every furry and smooth-skinned variety in the vicinity. The inner wall of the garage opposite the garage door was occupied by a spacious pine staircase which led up to two recently-built large bedrooms, affording the garage little use as a garage unless the staircase could be removed. By the lower step of the staircase was the third door into the kitchen, enabling one to do a complete circle within the house. This phenomenon greatly amused our seven-year-old daughter Tilly, as she could leave by one door of any room and appear at the opposite door with a delighted grin on her face.

We felt the two large bedrooms and balcony, which completed the first floor of the cottage, made our investment wholly worthwhile. Tiny floor-resting windows with single wooden shutters, enormous low central beams which only Tilly could walk under without ducking, steeply sloping roofs, and beautiful pine-finished ceiling and floors rendered the rooms delightful. A strange feature of the upstairs double bedroom was that, although the pine floor appeared solid, sound carried to the ground floor could be heard as clearly there as if that person was occupying the same room.

That first evening, oddities put aside considering the late hour, with unpacking to do, beds to make up and hunger to satisfy following a wearying twelve-hour journey, there seemed nothing so important as a hot meal, a bottle of wine, and bed.

Sleep and the dawn of a new day brought renewed optimism and an excitement that we could actually make our project, our investment, work. We adored France and six years of holidaying in Brittany, the Vendée, the Charente, the Var, the Auvergne and the Pyrenées had convinced us we were committed francophiles. One day while holidaying in the south of France we had been invited to visit a friend of my husband, who had bought a home in France, about an hour's drive from the coast. The house was part of the old quarters of a *vieille ville*. To reach it we had to climb the stone steps up to the centre of the town through to the covered quarters. The houses there were a tangled mass of old stone, where a floor of one house formed part of the roof of another. We walked beneath a dark archway and found ourselves facing a large arched corner doorway. This was the entrance to their house. A spacious lounge led towards tall French windows and a narrow balcony beyond, with a view of a small courtyard and the orange-tiled intermingling roofs of houses. A black iron spiral staircase led from a corner of the lounge to the three floors above, and eventually to an open rooftop. The house was so very different from anything we'd ever seen. That was the day I recall, in which a seed of fascination was sown within us for every aspect of French living.

The West Coast intrigued us. It had everything – golden sandy beaches, areas steeped in history, more than the average hours of sunshine, reasonable accessibility, and a serene, unforgettable beauty that appealed to us. In the summer of 1992 we arranged to spend two days in the Charente-Maritime and two days in the Vendée at the end of our summer holiday, solely devoted to searching for properties. The viewing arrangements had been made with estate agents in England, in liaison with their counterparts in France.

We'd arrived to begin our search at our hotel in Pons, an ancient walled city less than half an hour's drive from the pine-backed golden beaches of *'La Grande Côte'*, brimming with enthusiasm and anticipation. Rather strangely we had been asked to report to an estate agent at a small town an hour's journey inland by nine o'clock the following morning. We'd queried why there were no estate agents along the coastal side of the Charente-Maritime, but were reassured that the gentleman was a reliable contact and he would be able to show us properties in all areas of the coastal region. They had dealt with him on many previous occasions; he was excellent and spoke good English. As our journey inland progressed we grew more and more uncomfortable as we passed through villages of dilapidated, dusty buildings, many with permanently closed rotting shutters that had not seen a coat of paint for many years. Old ladies carrying *baguettes*, with sun-baked complexions and perplexed stares, and the occasional bedraggled barefooted child reminded us that the villages were inhabited. The roads were straight, deserted and interminable, cutting through endless flat uninteresting countryside, with field after field of maize and wilting brown sunflower heads. No one heralded our arrival at what was little more than a roadside village. Our map led us to a smart bungalow that appeared strictly residential and with no indication that it was anything other than exactly that. A kindly, white-haired lady answered the door, gave us coffee and explained that it was her son we'd come to see; she'd go and get him, he was still in bed. We were badly in need of refreshment so the offer of coffee was welcome; it gave us time to collect our thoughts.

A few minutes later a tall bronzed gentleman appeared at the garden gate. He spoke only one or two words of English and seemed slightly taken aback at our presence there.

"Er *quoi*, what do you *chercher*?" he faltered.

We tried to explain that we'd been told he would be able to show us some older-type character properties within our price range and within half an hour of the sea.

"Ah....!" He searched his drawer and produced two photographs of modern bungalows, very smart, completely lacking in character, and what was more important, both in the immediate vicinity. He could not help us, he smiled, registering our perplexed expressions, he only did properties in that area. The English agent had instructed us to ring them if we got into difficulties; we thought this was an appropriate moment to remind them of their offer. We had to find out quickly why there had been such a mistake. The bronzed gentleman offered to phone England for us and our lady who answered, on being informed of our dilemma, offered apologies, said she would speak to head office, find out what had happened, and ring us back. A few minutes and another delicious coffee later the phone rang again and a conversation took place in rapid French, then the phone was handed to us and we spoke to the gentleman from head office. The person we needed to see was Monsieur Gauthier in Gémozac. He would speak to the man in question and arrange for him to see us. In the meantime we should return to Gémozac and ring him when we arrived, just to confirm a time he would be able to see us. Gémozac was over an hour's drive, retracing our route over the countryside we'd driven through that morning. We thanked the bronzed gentleman and his mother for their hospitality and returned to the coastal regions or rather to Gémozac, a market town of some character.

It wasn't difficult to find the *centre ville* with its distinguished church spire, the magnificent *Mairie* and tucked away in a narrow street not far from the square, the *immobilier*. A whole half-day of our two days had been wasted, and there was more disappointment to follow. A telephone call to London revealed that Monsieur Gauthier could not see us until 16.00 hours that afternoon. We had four and a half hours to waste. There was little we could do but adhere to local tradition in the form of the sacred mid-day two-hour break in which to slowly savour culinary delights in the relaxed atmosphere of the local restaurant. We decided that afterwards we would explore the countryside around the town, try to get a feel of the area, the architecture and style of traditional buildings, generally spend the time usefully and try to keep our spirits up. The countryside was how we imagined it – narrow twisting country lanes, fields of vines, villages dominated by elegant Romanesque churches and stone troughs of delicate red pelagoniums.

At 16.00 precisely, Monsieur Gauthier greeted us warmly, first in French and then in English. He immediately set to work and showed us details of four properties, one with a neat garden, mature trees and a tiny well overflowing with red pelagoniums, an absolute delight but with an asking price that was anything but. My eyes lingered on the pretty cottage, the price quite out of the question, as too was the next property. The third, a white cottage with a long, low side wall entirely covered in Virginia creeper and neat red and pink roses growing at the front of the cottage, was new on the market. Only one other couple had seen it so far, and the cottage was owned by an English couple seeking a quick sale. The fourth was a neat semi-detached Charentaise house with a fitted kitchen and modern bathroom. Across the road from the side of this house was a panoramic view of the Gironde estuary. Having had a fruitless day of travel and disappointment, we agreed to view the two properties that at least would meet our finances. Monsieur Gauthier was happy to take us there himself using his car. He drove us across the square and almost immediately we were out of the small market town, driving rapidly in the opposite direction from the area we'd explored earlier.

Fifteen minutes later we pulled off a lane into a small hamlet, took a reverse curve along a grass track and pulled up by what appeared to be a 'cupboard' in the long low rear of a cottage.

"That's it," he announced, "I LOVE the garden."

Monsieur Gauthier tried unsuccessfully to open the 'cupboard' door, then we sauntered round to the front of the all-white cottage.

"The Engleesh, they paint everything white," he smiled.

We opened the garden gate on to a patio and tried the key once again in the patio shutters, this time with success. It led us directly into the lounge. All the rooms were spacious, the shower room primitive, the large kitchen almost entirely bare. The pretty garden with mature trees, a generous lavender bush, umbrella pine, a rose bed, hibiscus, a *lilas d'Inde* and a flourishing mimosa, was offset by pretty stone troughs, even a garden seat and a dry stone wall draped in white roses and ivy, and looking extremely enticing. Was it, however, what we were looking for? A garden would need constant attention, whereas a courtyard was more in line with what we'd envisaged. The cottage was roomy and rambling rather than cosy and would be difficult to heat in the chillier months.

As early evening was approaching we decided to postpone judgment until we'd seen the second property. We all piled into *monsieur*'s car and sped off towards the coastal road, where on turning an acute bend the magnificent sight of glistening white cliffs suddenly loomed into view to the right. These, explained Monsieur Gauthier, followed the original coastline. The fields opposite had all been reclaimed to form fertile agricultural land, and farms offering *fromage de chèvre* could be seen in the vicinity. Suddenly the road began to climb steeply until a full view of the estuary appeared, the water shimmering in the late afternoon sunlight. Here the road swung slightly inland and Monsieur Gauthier pulled up beside a pretty house situated end on to the road.

The house to be viewed was the semi-detached cottage furthest away from the road. The entrance led directly into a pleasant *salon*, at the far end of which was a short hall and leading off it was a kitchen, then a small modern bathroom and finally a double bedroom. The kitchen was fully fitted with magnificent oak floor and wall units. Above the sink were glazed windows, two feet away from a high stone wall, the top of which was completely hidden from view, cutting off all natural light to the kitchen, and necessitating permanent lighting arrangements, the effect of which was unbelievably claustrophobic. To view the upper floor we had to clamber up a loft ladder propped up in the hallway into a large gaping hole in the ceiling. The upper floor was completely unrestored, with only a temporary floor and three small window openings with shutters but lacking windows. It would cost very little to install three bedrooms into the roof space, Monsieur Gauthier reassured us. The small garden ran parallel to the far end of the building, out of sight from the house, but was such an overgrown tangle of blackberries, thistles and long grass it was impossible to inspect it. One would need the assistance of a mechanical digger before contemplating its use as a garden. An elderly French lady lived in the adjoining house we were told, so it was a very quiet spot. That tranquillity could well be disrupted if the occasional sudden influx of guest families with young children were allowed on the scene, we contemplated, at some cost to our friendship with the neighbours.

It was well into the evening by the time we arrived back in the Town Square. Monsieur Gauthier had extended his working day to accommodate us, and we felt very much obliged to him for his kindness. We said our thanks and good-byes, indicated that we needed time to think about what we'd seen, and returned to our hotel in Pons for dinner. Would we ever find precisely what we were looking for? Were we even doing the right thing? I lay on the bed, staring straight up at the chandelier, my head throbbing.

"You know," my husband interrupted the silence, "I rather liked the first house we saw."

"I thought you hated it."

"I thought YOU hated it."

"No – not really. It had definite possibilities."

The following morning we returned to the all-white cottage on the lane. Monsieur Gauthier had trustingly handed over the keys and allowed us to spend time there alone, vacillating over the practicalities of purchasing a property which fell short of our expectations, yet had exciting potential and was situated in an idyllic spot within a country hamlet of five very individual houses. The kitchen could easily be modernised and had oodles of space for fitted units. The shower room was an eyesore. Positioned as it was, it could neither be made elegant, nor due to its location within the house, could it be relocated. The garden was lovely but would be expensive to maintain during our absence. On the garden side of the back lane stood a pretty walnut tree, and an apple tree laden with fruit overhung the wall of the *gîte* behind, dropping fruit on to the grassy lane. We opened the garden gate and strolled out into the lane. Gently aromatic wild mint was growing by the side of the lane. The multicoloured roof of the cottage sloped fairly steeply up from the front of the building, then very gently downwards to ground floor level at the rear, which was most unusual. The multicoloured Roman roof tiles indicating weathering by sun, wind and rain, as opposed to plain terracotta tiles, we'd been told, were much in demand and very valuable. The lane curved acutely to the right at the end of the hamlet then dipped steeply down into a valley and climbed up again in the far distance before disappearing out of sight. An approaching tractor could be heard rattling down into the dip, at which point all sight and sound was lost until eerily it suddenly appeared again at the end of the hamlet. After a moment it disappeared round a bend in the road at the other end of the hamlet and the air once again was completely still. The ambience of the cottage that day, bathed in the mid-morning sun, was magical, enigmatic and quite stunning. In that moment we completely succumbed; the decision was made. We loved it. The rest was simply a formality. We busied ourselves taking photographs, measurements, weighing up possibilities, priorities, and contemplating all the consequences of our proposed buy.

Further formalities followed. The young owners accepted our offer. We cancelled our stay in the Vendée, and as we had to leave our hotel room in Pons, Monsieur Gauthier kindly allowed us to stay in a *gîte* he had made available for customers. Our stay at this comfortable *gîte* was marred only by the embarrassing malfunction of the electric loo the following morning when Monsieur Gauthier forgot to take the electricity supply off the time-switch, which had turned off the supply at midnight!

The following day, after grappling with the mountains of paperwork involved, we were invited by the vendors to return to the cottage and indicate what pieces of furniture and any other items we would like to purchase. They were planning to move to Central Europe at the end of September and there were few things they wished to retain. A list had therefore been compiled of all items they were prepared to sell along with their modest asking prices. The young couple seemed very amiable and over a few glasses of wine we chatted and agreed that apart from two or three items we felt weren't in keeping with the character of the cottage and personal items of sentimental value they wished to keep that most things would stay. We were quite unaware at this point that intoxication had somewhat impaired our judgment when it came to adding up simple figures, even given the assistance of a calculator. However many times we totalled up the cost in sterling of the house contents we found it quite impossible to arrive at the same figure. Eventually we managed in our inebriated state to agree upon a sum, although none of us really believed it to be the correct total.

The final visit prior to our departure from this haven of sunflowers and vines was to the local bank to open a French bank account, having agreed to work towards transferring funds over to France and signing the *acte de vente* on approximately 23rd October, 1992. It concerned us that the pound seemed to be losing ground against the French franc and we hoped we'd made our purchase just in time. We could not have anticipated however, that just over a month later there occurred what later became known as 'Black Wednesday' when sterling collapsed and Britain was forced to leave the ERM. With the bulk of the purchase money still to be transferred we estimated the amount of extra cash we would need to find to complete the deal. As the pound continued to slide we confided to our English agent that we might have no alternative but to consider cutting our losses and pulling out of the venture should the pound plummet further. At this point our agent came up with a magnanimous and generous life-saving offer. The company could make available to its clients a certain amount of francs at an earlier rate of 9.3 francs to the £1. The offer was limited to £30,000 worth of francs per customer. To set up the deal they would need our cheque, made out to their Clients Account, immediately. I had to admit I was more than a little nervous at the thought of passing on my life savings in the form of a cheque to a stranger I had spoken to on the phone, had never had the pleasure of meeting but whose reputation and twenty-five years' experience in the field had stood the test of time. We acknowledged that this arrangement could save us from serious financial difficulties, and accordingly we accepted the offer. On 6th October the final payment was handed over to our English agent to complete our purchase. We were elated.

The following two weeks saw frenzied activity in the household. We visited the market and bought material to make curtains, coverlets, tablecloths, cushions and lampshades for the cottage. These we hoped, would help to make the place feel comfortable, and all of which it had lacked with the previous owners, who had lived amazingly frugally, perhaps taking into account the temporary status of their work there. I spent hours attached to the sewing machine, frantically attempting to complete the work to coincide with our next visit to France at half term.

The days passed in such hectic productivity and disarray that before we realised it two weeks had gone by with no word from the agents informing us that the funds had been placed with the *notaire* in readiness to effect completion. Until one morning, that was, we received a call from Monsieur Gauthier's office asking when we would be sending the money. He seemed surprised when we informed him that we had handed over the money to the English agent some two weeks previously, but seemed to accept that everything was in hand and progressing satisfactorily. We received similar assurances from the English estate agent, who told us the money would be wired over in the next two or three days. The next contact we made with the English agents was a worried call the day before our scheduled departure for France. The money had to be sent through a bank in Switzerland, he explained. There was absolutely no cause for worry; the money would be delayed only two or three days. Yes, we would be able to have the keys to the cottage when we arrived in France; the delay would make no difference, we could still go down for half term and stay at the cottage.

Our very first day in the cottage was spent frantically making it appear lived-in. We pruned the large rose bush at the front. We weeded the rose bed, battled with eventual success to start the lawn mower and managed intermittently to cut the lawn, trim the grass verge and rid the side of the house of its fringe of nettles and wild flowers. At the rear of the cottage we trimmed the dead stems from the border of Japanese anemones, and freed the plants from the large nettles choking them. Inside the house we fitted curtain poles, put up curtains, fixed lampshades, and placed rugs on the floor of the lounge and bedrooms; the *gîte* was slowly coming to life.

The walls of the gallery at the top of the stairs consisted of stark brown hardboard; the surface area was relatively small, with low walls, which looked bare and uninviting. I had managed to pick up three rolls of end-of-range wallpaper at a reduced price. We set about the comparatively easy task of transforming the gallery into a picturesque and appealing area, at the cost of suffering concussion each time our heads accidentally hit the great beam running across it. Being extremely pleased with our first day's work, we were already planning our next task. Our daughter had busied herself collecting wild flowers in her little basket, and generally observing all the wildlife around. Whenever she came across a particularly interesting specimen we had to immediately stop what we were doing to share in her latest fascinating find.

That night there was one of those ferocious storms that occur infrequently. They start out at sea and suddenly blow over in an instant. We were grateful to be tucked up in a warm bed away from it all. Suddenly my husband Keith leapt out of bed startled. "I felt large drips on my face." He switched on a small lamp that stood on the floor by the side of the bed.

"The roof must be leaking."

We grabbed a large receptacle from the garage and moved the bed closer into the slope of the roof, to avoid the offending drips.

"Better tell Monsieur Gauthier in the morning. They told us the roof was OK."

Under French law a vendor has to make sure before selling a property that the roof is sound.

"Just as well it rained. We found out just in time."

Very shortly afterwards the raging storm passed inland and we all managed a peaceful night's sleep, the only evidence of our disrupted sleep lying in the bottom of the bucket.

By the following morning the storm clouds had disappeared and the air was clear and still. Today was the day we had been waiting for. Today all parties would sign the *acte de vente* and the house would finally be ours! We collected a freshly baked *baguette* from the village and ate a leisurely breakfast, savouring the wonders of French traditions, and the gentle beauty of the French countryside, of which we were now quite definitely a part. Our thoughts were interrupted at that moment by an urgent tapping on the kitchen door. It was Martine, appearing rather flustered. We offered coffee.

"Oh no – no *merci*. I came to say – WHERE is de money?"

CHAPTER TWO

CONFRONTATION

Martine stood there, bewildered yet unrecriminating. It was one of those peculiar moments, emulating the effects of ineptitude, deep pain and ignominy, occurring concurrently within us.

"Have you spoken to head office in London?" I asked.

"Yes, but they tell us nothing."

We had spent two days inadvertently providing visible evidence to the whole community that new owners had moved in and at the end of the day, the house wasn't even ours, it belonged to someone else. We had no right to be changing anything or bringing articles into the house, in fact we had no right at all to be there. We felt foolish, angry, and deeply worried. If the money was available, why had it not been sent? Suppose the agent had been affected by the monetary crisis and was on the point of liquidation. Suppose our funds didn't exist any more. The worst scenario now appeared a distinct possibility. Outwardly we tried to stay calm. There was still time – the money was obviously unaccountably delayed but would arrive shortly. We moved the conversation on to the happenings of the previous evening, the storm and the leaking roof. Martine laughed. This happened all the time, she explained. When there is a storm a strong wind can blow the rain under the convex arches of the Roman tiles and water then drips down from the ceiling. It was quite normal; we'd get used to it. The roof was fine. Unlike us, Martine seemed now to be taking it all quite lightheartedly and didn't seemed at all concerned about us continuing in the circumstances to remain at the cottage. Whether it was previous experience dealing with the London office, or our apparent naivity faced with adversity, or simply that they had never before experienced anything quite like this, something made them believe that we were the innocent parties in this situation. They were now convinced we had genuinely paid over the money, and we were allowed to stay in the cottage. The week came and went, and we returned to England, still with no money forthcoming.

The moment the first opportunity arose after our return to England I was on the telephone to the agent, demanding a step by step account of what had happened to our money. This was followed up by a registered letter to the company demanding tangible evidence that they had received the money, in the form of an official receipt for the cheque I'd deposited with them, the name and address of the third party the money had been lodged with in Switzerland, and a date completion could take place. This information was to be forthcoming by return of post. The gentleman who owned the company continued to reassure us categorically that the money was quite safe, but on all other details remained reticent, even derisory, merely assuring us that the money was on its way, and appealed for patience. My letter remained unanswered. We were now receiving daily telephone calls either from France, or from the owners in Central Europe, requesting news on the transfer of the funds. The owners were by now extremely anxious as they were having to pay rent on their new apartment and pay the mortgage on the French property at the same time. They were certainly considering suing the English agent. On our part, our anxieties stretched to an even wider sphere, not only to the loss of the cottage, but to our life-savings being suddenly wiped out. I decided to ask a member of the family to put in a computer check on the business side of the company. She promptly came up with the knowledge that there was a lawsuit being presented against the company and they were also in trouble over submission of tax returns. They had moved offices three times over the last few years. We had to conclude that the company could be in serious financial trouble. The picture was not looking good. Our over-riding priority now was to do everything in our power to force the agent to return the money.

Early one morning I set off for the London office. The element of surprise was essential and I was determined that I would not leave without either the money or an official undertaking that I would receive it within seven days. I arrived at the office only to receive yet another blow – the company had moved to another address two weeks previously, yet another fact they had mysteriously avoided imparting to us. Of the people I spoke to in adjoining flats and offices, only one person knew of their present whereabouts. The new address was about a fifteen-minute ride away on the underground, and I set off in yet more urgent pursuit. It was just after noon when I eventually arrived at the new premises. The new 'office' was a small room on the first floor of a modern building. As I climbed the stairs a gentleman hastily descending the stairs challenged me. They had gone to lunch, and wouldn't be back until just after two. Would I like to return later? Immediately I was drawn into a dilemma. Could this be the gentleman in question, or could he be a colleague who might well warn him a lady was anxious to see him, in which case he might take the precaution of slipping back early from lunch? I could then be told he was not in the office at that moment and the opportunity of a personal encounter would be lost. I had not made the journey in order to be fobbed off yet again. I had to be sure of meeting him face to face, and to do that, the office being locked, I had to stay put. I took out a sandwich, parked myself at the top of the stairs, and waited.

Shortly after two o'clock I heard voices on the stairs, and two gentlemen approached the office. One was a tall, slim man, with distinguished features, and a cultured voice that sounded instantly familiar. I stepped forward, addressing him by name, and asked if I might have a word with him. To my surprise I was immediately shown into the office. His face showed little emotion, his manner was entirely reserved, and he appeared calm and relaxed.

"You know why I'm here. I'm here to collect my money."

I struggled to appear calm.

"As I've already explained to you," he began, "the money is

on its way to a sorting bank in England from a bank in Switzerland. The delay is regrettable but often inevitable. I promise you the money is quite safe."

"Not as safe as it would be with me."

I was determined.

"It is MY money. I have no guarantee the money will ever be paid over. I would like my money, I would like it NOW, and I am not leaving without it."

He shifted uneasily.

"I haven't got your money. It is tied up in the system. If I had it I would give it to you. You just have to trust me. I promise you, you will have the money within a week."

It was hopeless.

"Then I want an official undertaking in writing now, to that effect."

He walked dispassionately over to the other table, where the other gentleman sitting by a word processor, appeared not to notice our conversation, and he whispered a few inaudible words. If the two of them were suddenly to get heavy with me, I contemplated, I would be totally out of my depth. A few minutes later the tall gentleman returned, clutching a letter, which he asked me to check through. The letter admitted trying unsuccessfully to arrange transfer of funds on our behalf at a favourable exchange rate, and undertaking to refund the original payment in sterling within seven days in order that we might make our own transfer. It also offered to compensate us for any exchange rate loss by paying the difference between the two rates. It was the best I could achieve. We arranged to meet at a French bank in central London in seven days time for the cheque to be handed over. I left with the warning that if he failed to honour the commitment we would be consulting legal advisors.

At the allotted hour I sat nervously on the luxurious leather seat by the entrance to the French bank inspecting every person who walked through the door. I sat for fifteen minutes before rising to my feet, pacing up and down, taking glances

At the allotted hour I sat nervously on the luxurious leather seat by the entrance to the French bank inspecting every person who walked through the door.

out of the window at the rain-soaked executive buildings and the failing light, then at my watch and the passing minutes. I simply knew, I could feel it – he wasn't coming. I was becoming noticeably agitated. A porter asked if I was all right. I asked if I might use the telephone. Surprisingly the English agent picked up the phone immediately.

"Where's the money?" I screamed down the phone.

"Oh – hello," he breezed, in his usual derisory manner. "I DID try to ring you this morning but you must have left. The cheque was meant to be here this morning but it didn't arrive. They may be sending it by courier."

I'd heard enough. I put down the phone and left the building, feeling infuriated and absolutely helpless.

A few minutes' walk down the road on my way to the underground tube station I spotted a police station. At the desk I asked if I could speak to someone concerning a case of fraud. A kindly police sergeant listened sympathetically to my story, then informed me that as I lived out of the metropolitan police area and the 'crime' did not originate there I should visit my local police station and see if they could do anything for me. The following morning I rang the local police. They took down details and telephone numbers, and told me they thought there was very little they could do apart from perhaps have a quiet word with the agent, in that way they could put a certain amount of pressure on him to do the right thing. Sometimes just a police presence was enough to spur people like this into action. At the end of the day I held out little hope that anything fruitful would come of it. The next day the police rang me.

"Did you say you'd made the cheque out to a Clients Account?"

I replied in the affirmative.

"If money is paid into a Clients Account he cannot by law take that money for his own use, and if the client requests the return of that money, he HAS to give it to you. I think we may well pay the gentleman a visit after all."

I can never overestimate the debt I owe to that enterprising police sergeant. The police duly paid him a visit, pointed out various irregularities and from that moment the wheels of fortune began slowly to turn in our favour. He agreed to pay back the money, indeed was still maintaining complete innocence in the matter. However it was a very worried man who insisted on us signing a document he had drawn up in consultation with a solicitor, arranging its delivery by courier. The document consisted of a covenant forbidding us to say or imply anything to the media, or publish anything that would be likely to discredit or damage his reputation or his service, before agreeing to repay any of our money. I wondered about the legality of this type of blackmail, and believed it could be easily challenged if necessary but admit that the thought foremost in my mind at the time was that if we did not sign it he would refuse to return our money.

Five days on I returned to the French bank in the city of London. It could well have turned out to be a repetition of my first visit. Nevertheless I was never going to give up. As I entered the bank foyer I immediately spotted a familiar lank nervous figure huddled on a leather bench seat in the short corridor which led from the foyer to the bank. He rose as I entered; his white raincoat giving him the sinister appearance of a special agent in one of those old post-war black and white cinema movies. Indeed the whole situation was akin to a scene from one of those movies.

"Have you got the money?" were my first words.

"Indeed I have. Do you have the covenant?"

I had purposely not put my signature to the covenant as a precaution.

"Yes, but first I need verification."

We moved to the bank counter.

"I'm sorry to trouble you but would you please take this gentleman's cheque, ring up the bank and ask if the bank will honour the cheque?"

The lady looked surprised, but seeing the large amount of money involved, did not hesitate. A few silent minutes passed, before she came over to the counter.

"The cheque is good."

She eyed the tall gentleman, who was doing his best to appear inconspicuous, seemed to sense the seriousness of the situation, and the cheque was handed back to him. I approached the porter seated at his desk in the foyer. He greeted me with smiles of recognition remembering the previous occasion in which we had met, and in view of which he was clearly taking the whole situation with exceptional seriousness. I asked if he would witness my signature on a document and he nodded, obviously enjoying being asked to participate in this unique cloak and dagger event, colouring his otherwise uneventful day. What happened next resembled an incongruous reinactment of the key scene in a movie. I handed the agent the document with my right hand and simultaneously took the cheque from him with my left hand. The total distrust on both our faces spoke volumes.

"Do let's try to put all this behind us, and if ever you feel in need of my help, please do give me a call," were his parting words. His face was pale and drawn as he hastened out of the double swing doors, and disappeared among the passers-by in the street. I felt in that brief moment what almost amounted to compassion toward the man who had so nearly cheated us out of our life's dream.

Minutes later the money was on its way to the *notaire's* bank account in France, together with the extra money we'd had to find to complete our purchase. This meant we'd have less money to spend in renovation and we'd have to be less ambitious in our plans for the cottage, or take our time and do things gradually as and when we had the money. We certainly hadn't come through this amount of stress only to abandon the project. It was as though a weight had been lifted from my back and I wept intermittently in a confused mixture of emotions for most of the journey home that day. I could not, on reflection, help but speculate to try to understand the intricacies of what had gone on in the agent's mind during those weeks of procrastination, derisory comments and feeble excuses. It could have been that he had partaken in what is known in certain circles as a *'château* deal' where a group of people requiring different currencies assembles together at a pre-arranged venue to agree a price outside the current exchange rate. This illegal procedure, which at the time had perhaps gone horribly wrong, bore consequences which would not have been foreseen, but the very existence of which would not have been in their interests to have had disclosed. The alternative that I'd prefer to believe was not the case, was that our funds had been used to prop up a company in crisis.

We were now more determined than ever to realise our dreams. The *acte de vente* was signed by proxy, in our absence, on 10th December, 1992, four months to the day since signing the *compromis de vente*. This took place to the profound relief of the vendors, Monsieur Gauthier, and Martine, who rang us up in great excitement at the event that was so nearly never meant to happen. It was a grey overcast day back in England but it was as though the clouds had suddenly parted revealing only blue skies and perfect sunshine. A letter followed, confirming the *acte de vente* had been signed and we were the undisputed owners of the property. The deeds would be held at the *notaire's* office, to await our instructions. It was the best Christmas present to each other, indeed the only one that we could possibly have hoped for. The *gîte* was finally ours.

CHAPTER THREE

FRAGILE BEGINNINGS

With Christmas over it was time to cease celebrating, face the practicalities of our newfound situation, and pay a visit to the January sales. Our intentions were no longer to have kitchen units fitted for us at the cottage, but to buy the units flat-packed in England and to fit them ourselves in order to save money. We'd taken precise measurements and had meticulously drawn up our own kitchen plan, using cut-outs on a scale drawing of the kitchen, then sketching each wall with the units in place. Although we professed to have only basic knowledge of carpentry we'd studied the subject in great detail and planned each move. We could follow the instructions that came with the units, we had accurate measurements, and with a little help with the plumbing-in of the sink, apart from the task being time-consuming, there should prove to be no real difficulty. We'd have to pay attention to details, such as remembering to buy continental adaptors for the plumbing on the sink. French plumbing used pipes of a slightly different bore to the English standard, therefore in order to plumb an English sink into the French outlet we had to make the necessary adjustments. We managed to purchase solid oak units at a very moderate price. Together with a sink, heavy bench tops, three pine chests of drawers, plus other redundant pieces of furniture and items we had in the house, these could all be shipped over to France in a part-load arrangement. The items included a standard lamp, cot, baby bath, bedside tables, a nest of tables, hanging rail, blankets and duvets, and would then arrive in time for us to commence work in the Easter holidays.

An English lady we'd met in Monsieur Gauthier's office, who occasionally worked as part of his team when interpretation of technical terms was required, and with whom we had become quite friendly, had offered to act as caretaker for us and generally organise local people to do work for us in our absence. This included gardening, cleaning, plumbing etc. She lived a fifteen-minute drive away from the cottage, spoke fluent French, had been accepted by the local community, was extremely knowledgeable about the area and local customs, and had been very kind to us during the first couple of days after we had decided to purchase the cottage. She would be there to meet the removal van and open up the cottage for the drivers to unload the goods. Every small detail had been taken care of in advance; the goods would travel as a part-load, and would be delivered one week before we arrived. The driver would telephone our contact as soon as the lorry pulled off the motorway, to inform her he'd arrived, then she would either escort the van to the cottage or the driver would follow our map, find his own way there and meet her at the cottage.

What we could not predict was the letter we received the day before the goods were due to be picked up, informing us the trip would have to be postponed because there was a delay in collecting the other part loads. We promptly picked up the phone and informed the company that we could not afford any delay as we had booked a trip to France the following week in order to install the units they were meant to be taking down for us. In that case, they explained, they were very sorry but they would have to cancel the job as they had no deliveries in the area that week. It was a bitter blow to be let down in this manner at such short notice, but surely, we thought, among all those delivery companies advertising their services in French property magazines, there would be one who could fit in an urgent part delivery. We were positive there were numerous lorries following the route to Spain. Southwest France was merely on the way. We spent the morning telephoning company after company, most of them requiring more notice, or offering delays of up to three weeks, but all of them unable to help us at that time. One firm was entirely sympathetic, regretted they didn't think they could do anything for us, but said they would deliberate the possibility of adding our goods to a load that was going to Spain. They promised to ring us back if they thought it was a possibility. I had no more names to contact, no sudden inspirations; we were entirely thwarted.

The following morning a call came out of the blue from the company who had mentioned they had a lorry going down to Spain. They were sure they'd have room for our items but they would need to pick them up that afternoon. That wasn't a problem; the goods were packed, numbered and already labelled. The chests of drawers were crammed full of smaller items; no usable space had been wasted. We were in business! That afternoon a young man driving an inadequate-sized van arrived to pick up the goods. He winced a little on seeing the length of the kitchen bench tops, and proceeded not unlike one who delighted in completing the most complicated of jig-saw puzzles, to successfully deploy these skills in performing the amazing feat of easing the last carefully-labelled item into the last square inch of useful space in the van. We furnished the driver with a map, and the name, address and telephone number of our contact in France. We then rang Veronica, our new-found friend in the Charente-Maritime, to inform her that the driver would contact her sometime the following evening, and that we would ring her back the day after to check that things had gone according to plan.

Having had doubts that our goods would ever arrive in France on time, we later learnt that they had arrived safely. The driver had pulled in to the motorway exit, albeit the exit beyond the correct turn-off, shortly after dawn the following day, having driven through the night. Veronica was in the bath when the call came through, but there had been little urgency, as the driver was about to tuck into a well-earned breakfast as he made the call. Veronica expressed amazement that consumption of breakfast had revived him to such an extent that he was able to carry into the cottage ten-foot bench tops and pieces of furniture single-handed! A tiny chip out of one of the bench tops, which necessitated a simple repair, was the only damage incurred. We were now becoming increasingly excited and confident about the ultimate success of our trip, and the idea of transforming the kitchen. I toured the local market stalls and bought small olde-world type flower baskets and bunches of heather, a pine mug-tree, and two pottery storage jars to decorate the bench tops after the completion of our installation.

During our first evening at what we could now with confidence call **our** cottage, we lit a huge log fire in the fireplace, which produced a warm, comfortable, soporific glow throughout the lounge. We'd travelled down in a car loaded with a two-seater settee and one chair from a flat-packed cane three-piece suite we'd just acquired, the third chair we'd had to leave behind on this occasion, for lack of space in the car. Both Tilly and I had been so enveloped in double cushions throughout the journey that our heads were practically touching the car roof. We unpacked the kitchen units, assembled the settee and chair and relaxed a little. There was time to deliberate on the amusingly odd sight of a seven-inch weed growing out of a space between the marble tiles in the lounge that had greeted our arrival, and the downy nest we'd spotted taking up a three-inch space in the post-box. Burning the enormous pile of cardboard containers that were rapidly accumulating in the garage area supplemented the rather meagre supply of logs and giant cones we'd managed to collect. We were mindful of an earlier warning that chimneys in France were to be swept once a year if insurance claims were to be valid in the event of a fire and we carefully studied our sketches of the kitchen in the warm glow of the fire.

The following morning shortly after the appointed hour, Philippe, a local *plombier* and a friend of Veronica's, arrived to inspect the toilet and the possibility of removing it and replacing it with a good old-fashioned flushing toilet. This, he smiled, was *pas de problème*. Before we'd comprehended quite how he would achieve this, the toilet had been removed, and was lying rather embarrassingly in the middle of the grassy lane by the kitchen door. Soon both Philippe and the van could be seen rattling off down the lane and disappearing out of sight. In the meantime, feeling at a disadvantage over our miserable lack of colloquial French, we set to work in earnest on our own comparatively menial task in the kitchen. This involved removing old wall tiles to the height of the kitchen bench from the wall between the sink and the old fireplace, assembling each unit and placing each completed unit into its approximate position for fixing on to the wall. This proved to be extremely time-consuming but rather diverted our attention away from any urgent need for the missing bathroom furniture.

Just as we were beginning to believe Philippe was playing a practical joke at our expense, a noisy van drew up to the kitchen door, and in walked Philippe complete with sparkling new toilet equipment and a broad grin on his face. In what seemed no time at all, compared to the heavy work we were making of our relatively minor task in the kitchen, we had the pleasure of seeing demonstrated, and being presented with our very own miraculously efficient flushing loo! Every few minutes someone would succumb to the temptation to try out our new toy. We hadn't realised that to change a toilet was a relatively straightforward task to those knowledgeable in such matters. What absolute luxury!

Our euphoria was short-lived, when mid-morning the following day we noticed a most disgusting smell filtering through the cottage, particularly pungent around the area of the garage door. Farmers were busy at work in the fields opposite. We knew they used various forms of fertiliser but this one was so obnoxious that it was stifling and extremely unpleasant. The source of the revolting odour had still not penetrated our reasoning, however, until later that afternoon, we were inspecting something in the garage when we noticed a slight overflow spreading from the area of what we had recently established was the cover of the *fosse étranche*. We had been rather horrified at the prospect of having a *fosse* encumbrant upon our premises, installed beneath the concrete floor of the garage. The whereabouts of the *fosse* was something we had not felt the need to discuss with the vendors prior to the purchase, but which with foresight should definitely have been studied at length before committing ourselves to the purchase. One seldom feels comfortable discussing sewage arrangements and it was probably for this very reason the subject had been omitted from the various conversations. We'd been told that collecting tanks needed clearing approximately every eighteen months and it was something we didn't have to worry about for a while. It certainly had not crossed our minds that it was something to make inquiries about in the infancy of ownership. Faced with the emergency of our current situation we seemed to have no alternative but to swallow our pride and descend on the one person who would know who to contact. We got in the car and drove into Gémozac.

"*Ah, Martine, nous avons un inundation. Il faut vider la fosse!*"

She smiled at our agitation.

"You do not have a hole? People make the hole in the side. *Alors*, it is bad that I tell you this."

She picked up the telephone and spoke rapidly, each phrase punctuated by a little giggle and a fleeting glance across to where we were standing, feeling very silly. Then she looked up.

"He will come tomorrow morning, the first visit."

We thanked Martine, made a feeble attempt to join in the mirth, but feeling acutely embarrassed by the whole wretched episode, retreated rapidly to the car.

True to their word, an enormous tanker pulled up in front of the cottage at 8.15 the following morning. The driver then backed it up to the garage door, and needing no prompting from us made his way immediately to the *fosse* opening. We had spent a miserable few hours being unable to flush the toilet or face opening either of the two inner doors leading to the garage. The flood had receded a little during the night. This did not lessen the unenviable task of having to remove a near-floating *fosse* cover that had no lifting hook. The cement was beginning to crumble at two of the corners, and with an old thick polythene sheet tucked beneath the cover and draped over the garage floor at either side as a primitive seal, this was the only means of lifting it. The gentleman showed no visible signs of being appalled by this discovery, and immediately set to work emptying the *fosse*. During the *vidange* another amazing revelation unfolded. The invoice he produced for us mentioned a volume of four cubic metres. I looked at the invoice, then at my husband. "The *fosse* is only four cubic metres in size!" We asked the gentleman how long we could leave it before it needed emptying again.

"*Alors, pour quatre persons – er, trois semaines...*"

Three weeks – at approximately £45 each time! He had to be joking, but his expression conveyed the utmost seriousness. Leaving us to assimilate the news, he shook each of us by the hand, nodded politely and drove off. We both rushed in unison to the *salle d'eau* to wash our hands, and suddenly this unbelievable discovery seemed hysterically funny, though we were left with little appetite for breakfast that morning!

Access to the *fosse* was just within the garage door. Adjacent to the garage was the *salle d'eau* and the toilet. Although the parcel of land immediately outside the garage door belonged to us, the area was just large enough to park a car comfortably. The garden opened up on to the opposite side of the house, which would exclude the provision of a septic tank. Drainage could not be achieved without digging up the rear or front lanes and laying pipes at ninety-degree angles round the house and into the garden, let alone attempting uphill drainage. We would have to seek advice on the problem; there seemed no easy option. We hoped a solution could eventually be suggested that would involve bypassing the present *fosse*, facilitating *fosse* clearance from outside the house. The stupidity of our eagerness to install a flushing loo without checking the *fosse* arrangements had simply compounded the problem. Placing a stone in the cistern to reduce the flush was merely a feeble gesture on our behalf to lessen the burden. The ecstasy of the flushing loo had become the agony of a possible further *inundation.*

Fortunately for us, assembling the fitted floor units in the kitchen went virtually without a hitch. Philippe assisted us by installing the sink, and the loud gurgling noise that accompanied the sink emptying caused by the sudden alteration in the calibre of the pipework, was something that we got used to after a while. Even the discovery that the outlet to the kitchen sink opened up into a stone-filled pit in the middle of the flower bed did not discourage us. On the contrary, the flower bed adjacent to the outlet contained the tallest, healthiest plants around.

Philippe later installed two new taps on the bidet, two new electricity sockets on the wall above the bench tops and an extra spotlight in one corner of the kitchen. When we realised however, he'd set the spotlight near the highest point of the sloping ceiling, so that the light barely reached the bench it was designed to illuminate, and one would have had to be adept at climbing a step-ladder (which we did not possess) positioned on the bench top, let alone be someone who did not suffer readily from vertigo, in order to change a light bulb, he was eventually persuaded to lower the light-fitment by a comfortable two metres. The holes resulting from this procedure remained unplugged and virtually inaccessible. We replaced the ancient cooker, bought a brightly coloured linen-backed plastic table cloth to cover the dreadful pink formica-topped table, repainted the table legs, and our new kitchen looked elegant and quite charming. We could all now take a break with a well-earned beer and a slice of homemade fruit cake. Philippe looked at the offering quizzically.

"Er – pooding?" he volunteered.

"*Eh bien – du gâteau ,*" we laughed.

"*Ah – c'est bon.*"

There was just cause to celebrate at last.

The problem of the *fosse* continued to haunt us. Several

builders were consulted to give their opinions on what could be done about it and most shook their heads in disbelief on encountering the present arrangements. Advice included installing an electric toilet, but previous experience caused us to eliminate that idea, especially in the knowledge that power cuts were regular occurrences in the country. Installing a secondary 10,000-litre tank outside the garage door was another option. The third option was to install a new smaller tank outside the garage door with a pump that would automatically switch itself on at intervals and pump raw sewage into the bottom of the garden, the idea of which did not fill us with much enthusiasm. Our assumptions were correct as far as the *fosse septique* was concerned; land drainage ruled it out as a possible option, unless we could acquire the strip of land that occupied the space between two of the houses in the hamlet, close to our garage door. The land, twelve metres by seven metres, was overgrown with bamboo, grass and weeds, and didn't seem to belong to anyone. In all honesty, we considered the *gîte* behind us would have a prior and more compelling claim to this land, presently having a difficult turn-in to reach their property and nowhere to park their car.

Worse was to come. Examination of the empty *fosse* revealed that the washing machine had been plumbed into it, depositing 100 litres of water each wash directly into the *fosse*, unnecessarily, and contrary to what one would have expected. It was customary for sinks, showers, bidets and washing machines to be drained into a *puits perdu,* or soakaway, similar to the one leading from our kitchen sink. Redirecting the outlet into the soakaway was not an insurmountable task, but was yet another problem to be put right. In the belief that merely by re-routing the outlet of the washing machine our immediate problems could be solved, we gave permission for this part of the work to go ahead. After all, four cubic metres or four thousand litres was not too tragically minute a space to serve one toilet. We would try it out the following season. The recommended option was the provision of a secondary tank to be used together with the internal *fosse*.

We wrote to Veronica, with whom we would eventually be liaising over this work, informing her of certain criteria we believed would be imperative if this work were to go ahead. These included stipulations that the internal *fosse* opening be permanently closed, and that the tanks must be emptied from the outside opening only, making provision for the *fosse* to be emptied when no one was on the premises. We suggested, mainly due to finances, the work be deferred until we were able to assess over a season the inconvenience of the present arrangement and the effect of redirecting the washing machine outlet.

We planned to return in the summer holidays, with a car load including the remaining item that would make up the three-piece suite. On this occasion we intended to combine jobs such as painting, with enjoying a real holiday there and generally taking in the area. Various relatives were invited to either join us or spend some time out there to hopefully keep the place aired and looking lived-in. Unfortunately some relatives often have a habit of offering assistance in a most impulsive fashion. One such companion was determined to rid our dry stone wall and stone trough of every sign of the ivy that had resisted every such well-meaning previous attempt at such drastic action. After toiling for three days, in soaring temperatures with every inch of her body covered in protective garments, looking rather like a comical bee-keeper, and enduring the worrying signs of suffering severe heat exhaustion, the task was proudly completed. A dry stone wall displayed in all its glorious nudity, such as had not been seen for many a year in *Le Petit Hameau*! Ivy, we were informed, was a weed that must not be tolerated and allowed to take over. The white climbing roses, which were being choked by the ivy, now hung in pretty trails along the top of the wall and were allowed to flourish unhindered. The stone trough, left with no protection from its coat of attached twine, broke up almost immediately. Similarly the wall, having resisted the wrath of years of sudden winter storms, suffered its inevitable fate when, three months later, it collapsed in three places during the first autumn storm.

Far from encouraging visitors to keep the cottage aired, our enterprising and industrious guest insisted upon keeping the shutters and window of her bedroom tightly closed during the entire two weeks of her stay with us, "to keep the stifling heat out". She did not feel obliged to open the shutters even for a photograph intending to show the cottage in all its sunbathed beauty.

Once a month, usually on the morning of the second, third or fourth Friday of the month, depending on the town being visited, the community gathered at the local *foire*, or extended market. This was usually a big event in the market towns, and the *centre ville* was barred to all traffic. Stalls lined every street in the town centre and visiting the *foire* was usually one of the highlights of our holiday. As well as the usual stalls carrying locally grown produce, there were stalls with local goat's cheeses, specialist *brioche*, fresh shellfish including *moules* and *huîtres*, a specialty in the area. These latter stalls often prompted me to recall the time we wandered around the harbour in La Rochelle and watched in amazement as the majority of the local people, even children of five and six years of age, tucked into *moules frites*, without any difficulty, at the open-air restaurants. Even I found mussels difficult to cope with. At the *foire* there were stalls of leather goods, jewelry, shoes, clothes, sweets, framed pictures, tapestry, rugs, plants and even livestock. It was difficult to explain to Tilly why she couldn't take home the gorgeous, floppy-eared chocolate-coloured bunny she drooled over, and she had to be content with a necklace consisting of her name written on a grain of rice enclosed in a glass pendant and hung on a chain. I was tempted to buy an oleander, an evergreen flowering shrub with beautiful pink blooms, but had second thoughts when the gentleman warned me I'd need to cover it over if there was a harsh winter. Other stalls displayed bottles and cases of *pineau des Charentes*, an aperitif produced in the local distilleries, made from unfermented

*Stalls lined every street in the town centre and visiting the **foire***
was usually one of the highlights of our holiday.

grape juice with added cognac, and a definite favourite of ours. It was explained to us that bottles should always be kept upright and always served chilled. We usually walked away from the *foire* loaded with fresh produce and various bargains on offer.

The unenviable task of sanding down and repainting the flaking windowpanes of the French windows and the two large windows facing the lane was well overdue. We counted seventy-eight small wooden panes in all, most of which had the minimum amount of paint remaining on them. The work required concentrated effort with a steady hand and the smallest sized paintbrush, avoiding the hottest part of the day and the full sun on the window. A daunting task, but well worth the effort. We couldn't help noticing that the French on the whole did not place the same significance on outside painting and one could very often spot an English-owned cottage by the reasonable state of its external paintwork. This we attributed to the fact that paint was prohibitively priced in France, of relatively poor quality and due to extended periods of exposure to the sun's heat, maintenance of outside *volets* was necessarily an ongoing commitment that few could afford. On this occasion we had taken paint along with us, and that included metal paint to eliminate the rust that was beginning to appear around the edges and vents of the metal fold-back shutters to the panelled windows.

An amusing and interesting discovery was the way in which sound could travel clearly in the channels provided by the arched Roman roof tiles. It was possible to stand at the top of the stairs, at which point we were so close to the roof tiles we had to duck under the roof beam, and hear clearly a quiet conversation taking place on the patio of the *gîte* behind us. It was as distinct as though they were at the other end of a telephone line, not seventy-five metres away. Once we discovered this strange phenomenon we managed to avoid listening in to conversations but couldn't help being intrigued by it.

Our intentions at the time of buying the house had been quite explicit. Our prime purpose was to provide a rural retreat, not too far from the beaches, primarily for our own use and enjoyment of sun, sand, French traditions, the food, the language and the unspoiled countryside. At times when we could not be there, avoiding winter months, we would allow others to share the pleasure, and a little of the cost of our country haven, by letting for a few weeks during the summer months, in the hope that part of the maintenance costs could be recovered. We took great pleasure in allowing others to benefit from the enjoyment of a *gîte* holiday. We decided we'd experiment by letting to friends of colleagues and for a modest fee that hardly covered the cost, in the light of the knowledge that the house was not yet as we would like it to be and in the hope that we might learn from the experience. So when a friend contacted us who knew someone desperate to take his young family away on holiday but felt he'd left it too late to find anywhere, we believed this to be an opportunity to experience the joys and pitfalls of letting.

We'd already had some insight of what we were expected to provide for our guests when we'd arranged to be inspected with a view to possible future letting by a self-catering holiday home company. The lady arrived five hours late having had a two-hour drive south. She then proceeded to pull the place apart by insisting we had bars on the upstairs windows if they were to let to families with children, asking us to provide a microwave, and a larger double bed, as in her opinion the double bed was a little too narrow. She then quite unexpectedly announced that the house was very nice and they would accept it in their brochure the following year but with the proviso that there were no families with young children. This was disappointing as, being so close to the beaches, we felt that the cottage mainly appealed to families with children, and we were not at all happy with this arrangement. Eventually we reached a compromise. We would provide chains for the shutters of the upstairs windows for use with families that included small children, so that people could if they wished allow the shutters and windows to remain open approximately five inches for air at night. This would avoid the possibility of an accident, but we could still retain uninterrupted views of the countryside by avoiding bars on the windows.

The final few days of our summer holiday were spent frantically preparing for the very first family of visitors due to follow us in. We had provided typewritten notes on things to see and do in the area. We had generally spruced up, painted, made safe, de-cobwebbed, 'Pledged' and 'Eau-de-Javelled' upstairs and down. The previous owners had placed light-fittings into wine bottles as their only source of light in the *salon*, and this gave us the idea of making rather more glamorous lamp stands using the same principle. We had covered the bottles with Polyfilla, allowed this to set a little, then placed dainty yellow shells Tilly had collected earlier from the beaches at Ile d'Oléron over the surface of the Polyfilla, each slightly overlapping the next. The whole, when set, had been covered in clear varnish and made a rather effective-looking lamp stand. A straw-coloured shade completed the new look. We completed a further lamp in this way, this time using little shiny coloured pebbles collected from the beach at Antibes. The two lamps were taken out of their boxes and placed in strategic positions in the lounge, giving a homely feeling to the room. Similarly we had made two framed pictures of shell patterns, using a selection of shells collected from the beaches of the Vendée, using deep frames with glass backings. These were displayed around the *salon*.

So nervous were we that the family would not like the less than perfect cottage we spent a final anxious two days rushing around like demented fleas hopping from job to job, indulging in unnecessary self criticism. We needn't have worried. The family was so grateful to have a roof over their heads they found the cottage delightful and were extremely appreciative, even amused by the frequent encounters with an exceptionally friendly field mouse.

Closing up for the winter was a laborious task. All linen

needed to be washed and placed in mouse-proof storage bags. Very often the weather broke in early November; it could be unpredictable, often raining for days, and on the whole not conducive to dealing with mountains of wet linen, tidying the garden and attempting a final mowing of the lawn. Garden furniture had to be brought in, cushions and seat covers removed, lampshades covered and incidentals put away in drawers. Anyone having the misfortune to suffer visitors in the final few hours before departure would understand the chaos that ensues, when even offering a cup of coffee can be a major inconvenience. The water mains had to be turned off, pipes emptied, the toilet tank emptied, all doors and windows closed, secured and bolted and mouse boxes laid. With the final extermination of the pilot light, closing of gas cylinders, turning the electricity off at the mains, one naturally felt exhausted and hopelessly equipped physically to undertake a twelve-hour journey to the UK!

CHAPTER FOUR

THE LEARNING PROCESS

Correspondence with the travel company who had agreed to include our advertisement in their brochure the following year had proved to be irritatingly unproductive. We watched as other companies' submission deadlines came and went. When it was too late to include our advertisement in any other brochure, they wrote informing us they would be willing to include our cottage in their advertising brochure providing we drastically lowered our rental prices, and gave us a three-day deadline in which to return the signed contract. We contacted the company informing them that we'd based our prices on their assessment of a *gîte* situated in the same hamlet as ours, that didn't have three bedrooms, a separate kitchen, or a country view. Their guarded response to this enlightenment was that they would need to study their dossier on the aforementioned *gîte*. Eventually they reluctantly agreed to allow us to keep what we had considered were very reasonable prices. There was confusion too, as to what were the duties of the caretaker, and those of the company's representative. As the company took a massive 33 per cent commission on their high season lets it was obvious that some of the duties previously allocated to Veronica must now be transferred to the representative. Those duties included visiting the clients and to some extent trouble-shooting, which the company were keen to undertake. This left grey areas and naturally Veronica wished to have her particular duties clearly defined, which was not easy.

Finally the brochure arrived, displaying their own perversely unflattering photograph of the cottage, taken from the bare-walled garage side of the house rather than picturing it from the creeper-clad garden side. The accompanying map reference gave the reader the impression the cottage was situated well inland instead of close to the beaches and the schedule stressed its unsuitability for young children. *Ces grandes fautes* resulted in an abysmal lack of interest in our property and manifested itself in one solitary two-week booking by mid-March.

By the time Veronica returned from a trip to England and had a chance to check over the house, the gas service she had been trying to arrange since we'd mentioned it in October was well overdue. There was barely time to include it before the first 'official' company guests would arrive, and of course a far more pressing matter had arisen. Sadly we were paying the toll for closing up the cottage during the winter months. The house was showing signs of being badly affected by the heavy winter deluge of rain. The walls of the *salle d'eau* were covered in fine speckles of grey mould which proved impossible to remove by any conventional means. Philippe was dragged off by the panic-stricken Veronica to do a hasty room redecoration, including the toilet cubicle both inside and out, which he completed with determined verve if not with finite care. No one had cause to make a fuss when it was noticed that all pine accessories, hooks and light fittings were lightly smeared with cream paint. The garden was transformed yet again from jungle into garden with sweet smelling roses in two days, and the house again had a seven-hour invasion of cleaning lady with mops, buckets, cleansers and sprays. Never again were we to close all the doors to keep the rodents out. The effects of the air being unable to circulate within the cottage had proved to be far more dramatic and extremely costly.

As for the rodents – they had managed to find their winter refuge anyway, as we discovered at further cost. Part of the plastic piping along the edge of the chair cushion had been nibbled away by hungry mice. Some friends of Veronica who had been staying at the house in June had reported finding mouse droppings in the bed, and a family of invading mice had made their home for the winter among the blankets in the cupboard. In the rush to make preparation for the onslaught of visitors, cupboards had been opened and flicked through but not emptied, and bed coverings turned back and sniffed at, however such hasty examination had failed to spot the unwelcome visitors, to Veronica's immense embarrassment. The offending bed linen was removed and taken away for laundering and the whole incident made light of.

A further happening during their stay, this time leaving us the guilty parties and the ones feeling acutely embarrassed, was when our visitors had a visit from the local *gendarmerie*. They had called to repossess the television set for non-payment of the television licence. Fortunately Veronica happened to be visiting her friends at the time and decided to avoid any difficulties by paying the licence fee plus the fine on our behalf, a mere 837 francs. She was blissfully unaware at the time however, that we had been unable to decide whether to leave the television at the house, or remove it in view of the dubious cost-effectiveness of the small amount of time it had in use, against payment of a relatively very high licence fee. Knowing the television was not in use at the time anyway, we had failed to see the urgency and had delayed paying the fee until this could be decided upon. Realising that with people staying in the house, possibly using the set, we'd better pay the licence fee, the week before the incident we had therefore posted off the due amount to *Audiovisuel*. In the meantime we were unaware they had sent a reminder to the cottage warning of the consequences should we be in default of payment. This reminder was still in the post box, now revamped and installed in its new position on the rear wall of the cottage. The guests had felt no compulsion to open the post-box, and had found the whole occurrence hilarious. Veronica, however was not so amused. It took a whole year of telephone calls, letters, threats and visits before they at last lifted their unyielding objections and decided to refund one of the licence fees, and she vowed never to do anyone such a favour again.

The gas service was eventually arranged two days before the arrival of the company guests. Five minutes into the service the engineer announced that the water heater was dangerous and should really be condemned but, with an alarmed Veronica pleading and offering basic encouragement, he agreed to do his best with it. It had taken almost eighteen months of persuasion to accomplish a visit; the news was indeed ill-timed. Even more ill-timed was its eventual demise a few days later when our important guests turned on the hot water tap to an accompanying flash and a bang and an urgent message to Veronica that the water heater had blown up. Veronica's swift action and fortitude in a real emergency was one of her endearing qualities. Although bad fortune seemed to be attracted to her all her life like butterflies to buddleia, with each crisis the adrenalin flow would see her fly into action almost immediately, and each new crisis brought its own personal toll to bear on her. A phone call to the engineer brought the unsurprising news that no more temporary repairs could be attempted and a new heater was required. Worse still, he was having difficulty locating a new one. A third phone call revealed the news that a new apparatus had been found but they were having to send it all the way from La Rochelle, over an hour's drive away. It was then left to the enterprising Veronica to gently break the news to the unfortunate visitors that everything possible was being done that could be done but that they could be without hot water for another couple of days. Being in the position of managing other properties in the area she was also able to offer them alternative accommodation until the water heater could be fixed. The offer was much appreciated but they explained they were well settled and didn't wish the disruption of uprooting themselves in the middle of their holidays, realised what had happened couldn't be helped, and that the important thing was that everything was being done to rectify the problem. Whilst we were helplessly tearing our hair out with worry over five hundred miles away, the family were enjoying the rest of their holiday with a frivolous *"c'est la vie"*. The water heater was duly replaced with a brand new one and the hot water restored, thanks to Veronica's prompt action. The family's casual attitude to what would have been a preventable disaster had the engineer made himself available sooner was really quite astonishing, and they were later offered a substantial discount on another holiday, which quite understandably, was not taken up.

The company representative had not surprisingly, made herself suitably scarce during the heat of the crisis. She could not be relied upon to seize the bull by the horns and deal with a crisis situation given that both she and her equally elusive colleague were responsible for the whole of the Charente-Maritime and lived a two-hour drive away. On our part, having to pay for costly elusiveness was a luxury we could not afford. Indeed, having to pay for elusiveness, inefficiency and complacency on their part was something we could not continue to equate ourselves with. We felt we should justifiably sever ourselves from the company and venture out alone.

From feedback we had already received it was obvious that we'd have to provide more precise instructions for the washing machine, water heater, and toilet flushing. The washing machine occupying space in the *salle d'eau* had to be plugged into a special socket in the downstairs bedroom. Apart from the inconvenience, meandering cables were not conducive to safety with young children on the premises, and something would have to be done about it. The toilet flush was a continental lift and release type – extremely efficient if used properly, costly if inadvertently neglected through ignorance. On occasions when folks had naively lifted but pushed the flush in again, water had continued to flow without reaching any cut-off point until flushed again, sometimes running entirely unnoticed and with dire consequences allowing the *fosse* to accidentally fill up in just a few ill-fated hours. There was a request for an 'idiot's guide' on how to find the house, as it seemed that people were quite incapable of following simple instructions after a long and tiring journey. One person had even tried to force the patio door key into the door of the big barn, one of the other homes in the hamlet, with sand-blasted natural stone walls that bore not the slightest resemblance to the detailed description of our white cottage. Hours of driving made people weary and clouded their judgment to the extent of them being unable to assimilate anything other than the simplest of basic directions.

The barn was a magnificently audacious building with tiny windows and varnished shutters that towered like a regal giant over the rest of the buildings. It was owned by a family who regularly made the five-hour trip from Paris to their country residence, being one of the three French-owned properties in the hamlet. Tilly would regularly delight in bounding up to their daughter who was older by one year, with a cautious and rather anglicised *bonjour* that would inevitably be met with an embarrassed and bemused stare. The two *voisines* were unable to strike up anything approaching an enduring friendship however, as the conversation was not able to progress beyond the initial *bonjour* and the two were left imprisoned in a world of giggles, beckoning and mime. The family soon tired of the time-consuming journeys to and from Paris, sold the house to enthusiastic and committed – if a trifle eccentric – English francophiles and returned to the urban life from which they had never really become detached. The new owners Tom and Annabel adored France and their new purchase, were full of enterprising plans and revelled in their new surroundings. Their wonderful sense of humour, generosity of spirit, and zeal for life endeared them to everyone in the community. These qualities were very soon put to the test when shortly after they moved in Annabel's face appeared at the other side of the stone wall.

"Do you know where we can go to get the *fosse* emptied?"

Later her face appeared at the wall again.

"You're not going to believe this..."

One of the barn's most impressive rooms was the luxury bathroom, with rose-coloured two-tone toilet, deep bath, matching bidet, basin and beautiful tiled floor. Incredibly all the effluent from this esteemed porcelain quartet drained through a total absence of even the most primitive of plumbing into a miserable channel, which led to a homemade *fosse*, namely a hole in the ground. The previous owner, who apparently used to pump out the sewage regularly himself, was envied among the community for his dedicated care of the lushest lawn around. Crucially Tom and Annabel had learned too late the lesson of most aspiring would-be property owners in France, one that very few bargain or budget for. The installation of a QE2-sized *fosse septique* replaced the installation of a swimming pool as their number one priority and all were able to breathe freely once again.

Of the two remaining French-owned properties in the hamlet, one belonged to an elderly lady who was presently living with her daughter in a nearby hamlet. The house was behind the central green patch on which stood a garden seat beside a dainty tree, and centrally a mound of rocks and a pretty stone *moulin* complete with sails. She it was who used to tell the occupants of the houses which of the *champignons* they had gathered could be eaten and which were poisonous and should be discarded. The 'green' in front of the house, enjoyed by all the occupants of the hamlet, was part of her land, as were a variety of pockets of land and outbuildings scattered around the hamlet including the area occupied by a stone shack at the bottom of our garden. By the time we had taken possession of the cottage, the frail old lady had abandoned her house and moved to her daughter's. Shortly afterwards she died, and about a year later a new French family moved in.

The largest residence in the hamlet, known to everyone as simply *la grande maison blanche*, was a beautiful old house with bottle-green shutters set in acres of ground. Beyond the house was a formal wood of poplars planted by the French owners shortly after they bought the house in 1935, a lake dug out with their own hands, and an orchard. The couple lived and worked in Royan, a twenty-minute drive away, and their weekend residence was their pride and joy, lovingly cared for by these gentle folk. Most weekends in the summer Monsieur Dibon would be seen happily jogging along seated on his motor mower. Not

Every evening before dinner M Dibon and his wife would stroll along the lane with their dog, past the gate to the patio where we would be dining, and call out a breezy 'bon appétit' in passing.

content to spend the whole day fastidiously cutting the grass on his own many acres, he would be unceremoniously shearing the grass verges, central green and rear lane of the whole hamlet. Every evening before dinner he and his wife would stroll along the lane with their dog, past the gate to the patio where we would be dining, and call out a breezy *bon appétit* in passing. Two years after we became their near neighbours the esteemed Monsieur et Madame Dibon gave up the struggle to maintain what was becoming an increasing and intransigent burden on their efforts, resources and time and put the house up for sale. The day they signed away, to an American gentleman and his British wife, their beloved country refuge which had survived the Second World War, and in which they had brought up their children, the pen shook with uncontrolled emotion. All recollection of the occasion blurred into a suffusion of tears, at their profound and indelible loss.

Later we learnt that the new owners had inherited fascinating framed photographs of the building as it existed when the house had been bought in 1935, a mere shell in comparison to the building as it stood today. Only the ground floor of the amazingly substantial house had been lived in, the upper floor remaining largely unrestored. The massive and impressive lounge, which ran the whole width of one end of the house, had three pairs of French windows along one long side, offering magnificent views over the acres of rolling land and the formal poplar wood beyond. A beautiful open fireplace dominated one end of the lounge, and the most magnificent and substantial polished hardwood dining table I'd ever set eyes on stood as a striking centrepiece to the room. The new owners whose intention it had been to buy a small flat in the south of France, had by chance driven past the place, fallen in love with the house and had rashly become unintentional owners of the revered property.

The garden gate of the fifth house making up the hamlet opened into the grassy lane directly behind our cottage. A pretty cottage with red climbing roses growing profusely across its side wall, it was the most secluded of all the properties in the hamlet. It was one, which, apart from a loo permanently blocked somewhere between it and the *fosse septique* that had fooled every plumber appointed to deal with the problem, boasted fewer crises than the others. Even the garden was laid mainly to grass with the occasional shrub. Owned by an English couple with a French name they lost no time in informing us almost as soon as we were introduced that they were about to sell the cottage to free finance they felt could be better used elsewhere. By studying the current property market they estimated it could take them up to two years to sell, and strolled off expecting to see us in the summer. The house however, attracted a ready buyer almost immediately and by the summer we were introducing ourselves to the new English owners, a quiet couple whose love for the area seemed to grow with every passing moment they spent there.

While the owners behind us would spend much of their day enjoying themselves stretched out on sun loungers we just couldn't seem to get it together sufficiently to be able to down our garden forks and trowels and spend time relaxing in the garden. Although we were spending a fortune paying a gardener so others could enjoy the *gîte* we did not allow the same such luxury for ourselves. Inevitably the first day of our stay would be spent in the garden, mowing, trimming and weeding it into something of an acceptably satisfactory state. We decided at length that it would be appropriate, looking at the appalling state of our finances after the disastrous summer with the holiday company, to try to look at ways of saving ourselves work and reducing our colossal maintenance bill.

Ours was the only *gîte* in the hamlet with beds to weed; we had a rose bed and a flower bed both requiring regular maintenance. The flower bed was for the most part neglected and messy, with a single prolific but woody lavender bush taking up one corner of it. This, we decided, would be a herb garden. We spent a whole morning clearing the bed and replanting it with rosemary, thyme, sage, marjoram, mint and chives. More herbs were planted in the stone troughs. Wood bark was the answer to our weeding problems we believed. It was cheap and could be bought at the local supermarket – until **we** arrived that was, and cleared all stocks of *écorces* from all the supermarkets within a ten kilometres radius. We emptied ten bags on to the rose garden alone and returned twice for more, but at the end of the day it looked terrific and entirely appropriate, and we surveyed our work with pride.

Next we roped up the very large rectangular stone that had been taking up valuable space in the garage and dragged it round into the lane, through the garden gate on to the patio. Similarly two smaller square stones were removed from the garage and placed in position on the patio and the large stone heaved up and cemented into position over the smaller stones to make a small stone bench. This we perceived would take some of the pressure off use of the garden seat, a long bench type seat made almost entirely of white wooden slats with cast iron legs and supports. The ongoing problem we faced with this was that the seat took a lot of abuse and on each successive visit we had been obliged to replace at least two of the slats. At forty-five francs per slat we worked out that for the eight slats we'd gradually had to replace in two years we could easily have bought a new bench seat – *mais tant pis*, as they say.

Another irritating problem involved the drainpipe running down the front corner of the cottage. The lower edge of the pipe was severely dented and twisted causing water to be directed into the corner of the house, compounding the effect of damp in the ground floor bedroom. The problem was easily corrected by simply replacing the dented lower section, directing the lower outlet outwards and allowing the water to run along two upturned tilted Roman tiles and down along the side of the lane. The dampness on the bedroom wall improved almost immediately, although there still existed the problem of the carpet. We continued to make futile attempts to eliminate the offensive odour by shampooing, vacuuming, airing, even burning scented candles in the room but finally recognised that the well stuck down carpet needed to be earmarked in the not too distant future for major surgery.

One morning an over-friendly, slightly obnoxious Englishman approached us on behalf of the new owners of *la grande maison blanche*. They were at that time providing a fine shingle covering for the drive leading to the entrance at the side of their house. As this bordered the parcel of land in front of our garage he wondered if we would like that area smartened up at the same time. The workmen would remove all the weeds and cover the whole area with shingle, at the relatively small cost of 750 francs. Remembering the times we'd plodded through mud and weeds to unlock the garage door we agreed that it could only enhance the area. Within a few minutes a lorry-load of shingle arrived, we handed over the payment to the man and the lorry emptied its contents over the area, mainly on the drive side. No one attempted to remove the weeds, the parcel of land adjoining the garage was barely covered, and we never saw the little Englishman again. We were, however, reminded of the incident a year later when the lady owner of the big house joked about the time when she'd bought a large stone pot to cover the stump of a tree she'd had to have removed as it was growing too near to the house. She'd ordered a bag of shingle to place in the pot, must have got her French words mixed up and had been horrified when a lorry-load of shingle had arrived, but had at the time dismissed the incident and asked the gentleman to throw it over the drive! We were too embarrassed to tell her how her greedy English supplier had made a hefty back-hander out of the mistake, and how we'd been taken in by him. She would have been most upset by the incident.

The disastrous summer bookings had convinced us that removing the middle man was the preferred route to follow. This meant much of the responsibility fell upon us as owners to design and provide colour brochures, booking forms, schedules, report sheets, invoices, and directions for holiday makers, and we set to work accordingly. The advertisement had to be submitted to a good magazine in which holidaymakers were invited to book directly with the owner. Success of the operation depended on the services of a good caretaker and a good working relationship between the two. Veronica had been beset with problems of her own – a clinging next door neighbour who wished to be escorted everywhere and would not leave the village except on the front seat of Veronica's car. She would sit behind a curtain waiting to accost Veronica the moment she returned from an excursion without her, demanding where she had been, and why she'd been gone so long. She was having ongoing problems with a new woodburning stove she'd bought and had installed by a local tradesman. The stove aspired to backfiring periodically, sending billows of black smoke into her *salon*, terrifying visitors and infuriating the host. All attempts to persuade the tradesman to take responsibility for the installation had failed, the tradesman shifting the blame on to a faulty chimney that happened to bend the wrong way causing smoke to be blown back into the room when the wind blew in a certain direction. Veronica could not picture herself somehow standing at the door of her cottage holding up a handkerchief to check the wind direction before making the momentous decision whether or not it was safe to light the stove. The *maçon*, on the other hand, insisted the chimney was fine and the apparatus had not been installed properly. With a court case imminent against the tradesman involved Veronica's nerves were taking something of a battering.

Veronica's routine meant that she spent the winter in England and the summer, March to October, in France, and she would be willing to cover the whole season for us. Ideal – or so we thought until we discovered after offering someone the two Easter weeks that she had commitments in England and would not be returning to France until April. Fear not, she pointed out heroically, she had a very good friend who was always willing to cover for her during an absence. As she had committed herself to the whole season, which she admitted she'd thought of realistically as being June to September, she would go over earlier in the year. She would take her friend over to the house, show him the ropes, arrange for the house to be cleaned, give the gardener a ring to remind him of the dates he should tidy the garden and cut the lawn, and all would be well. Until, that was, the situation began to get more complicated, when her friend suddenly announced that he would be coming over to England for Easter that year. Undeterred by this sudden setback, Veronica explained that she would check the house, leave a welcome note for the visitors, leave them the telephone number of another friend of hers in case they got in to difficulty and give them the date her original friend would be returning. Everything would be fine, she reassured us.

The Easter visitors, as it happened, had an unexpected heatwave as well as unexpected visitors, and thoroughly enjoyed their stay, in spite of having to dispose of the couple of dead mice occupying the kitchen floor. They were especially pleased as they were a large family who had rented the *gîte* for little more than the cost of two *vidanges*.

By the time we arrived in late May one other week had been rented out and we arrived at the end of their week, rather horrified to discover that many of our oak kitchen cupboard doors had begun to warp at the joints and would not close properly. Presumably this occurrence resulted from damp on the inside walls of the kitchen behind the cupboard doors, over the winter period. Eight doors were affected and we would have to contact the suppliers, as this should not have happened. Hopefully the doors would be covered by the five-year guarantee, in which case they would need to be returned to the UK and replaced. The discovery meant we would have to review our winter closedown procedure and adopt a new routine of leaving all the kitchen cupboard doors open to minimise the build-up of damp behind the doors.

We had heard disturbing reports of Monsieur Gauthier passing the house in mid-May to find the shutters and window open and the place apparently deserted. He had propped the window closed with a large stone and reported the incident to

Veronica, who sent her cleaner to check the house. She reported that not only was the window open but the door to the garden was also open. As the cleaner was basically an honest if simple-minded lady, Veronica felt she had no reason to disbelieve her. She also told Veronica that the house had been very dirty when the Easter visitors left and she had spent four hours cleaning it, making sure it was securely locked up before she left. By the time we arrived the mystery had deepened. We took the usual meter readings only to discover they were very little changed from the previous report and no one appeared to have stayed at the cottagee. On the other hand, it was extremely untidy – coat hangers were strewn over the bed, the clothes rail from the upstairs bedroom was in the *salle d'eau*, dirty crockery lay strewn in the kitchen and generally we wondered what on earth had been going on.

We rang the gentleman in Mortagne who had been standing in for the absent Veronica and invited him over. Eventually a very strange individual arrived clutching a tiny hound on an excessively long lead and introduced himself as Veronica's friend. Although the man was English he insisted the hound could only understand French and spoke incessantly to it in short sharp sentences of *"Viens toi"* or *"Attention, Frou-frou!"* He could offer no explanation as to why the cottage appeared in such a state, apart from explaining he had not checked the place before we arrived, as he knew we were coming and would check it ourselves. We explained our concerns that the visitors appeared not to have stayed there and he casually agreed that it certainly looked that way. Our exasperation was beginning to surface. Had he paid them a visit during their stay, we asked. No, he had not been asked to. He seemed not only entirely detached and unconcerned about the matter, but appeared to distance himself from all responsibility regarding the visitors' welfare. Only later, over a beer on the patio, did we ascertain that he'd come over to France after suffering a nervous breakdown. He told us he still suffered occasional memory lapses. Only recently he'd had a call from his father who was at Bordeaux airport waiting to be picked up; his son had completely forgotten he was arriving that day. He'd been a priest in England, he volunteered. He had for some time been plagued with doubt about his vocation in the church and one morning had stood before his congregation rigid with terror and soaked in perspiration wondering just how on earth he could possibly get through the service that morning. Following his breakdown the bishop had decided his harrowing experience was a sign that he should take time out, spend a few weeks with friends in France, relax, recover and try to discover where his true vocation lay. Months later after making a slow recovery in the easy atmosphere of a country more attuned to basic living, he decided to make his permanent home in France.

Veronica, too, had left her job after suffering severe nervous exhaustion and had found solace in the French countryside. The occasional relapse while under pressure or faced with a particularly stressful situation was known to have happened. The present situation was more than enough to dispatch the most stoic of mortals into a state of morose depression. We wondered if they had met coincidentally or whether like sufferers were drawn to like. What was in no doubt was that this poor wretched vestige of a gentleman was quite unsuitable a person to be put in charge of the cottage.

To this day no satisfactory explanation has been offered to explain why the door and window of the cottage were left open. Veronica preferred to believe that someone found the keys and broke in to the *gîte*, but nothing appeared to have been taken and this kind of petty crime was very rare in France. After our afternoon conversations about memory losses and breakdowns we were inclined to proffer our own theories on the matter.

At some point during our stay we took the precaution of purchasing a new washing machine. The machine we'd inherited was definitely beginning to show signs that it might well suffer in the not too distant future the same fate as the water heater, something to be avoided at all costs.

Two weeks after we returned to England we received a tele-phone call from the lady who had booked the cottage for the week prior to ours. They had arrived very tired late in the evening, she explained, had decided the cottage was not for them, had therefore returned the keys and had continued on to a bed and breakfast hotel. They wondered if we would mind returning the rental money, as they had not actually stayed there. There was a stunned pause in the conversation before I eventually replied. What was the reason for such a request and why had she left it so long to contact us? Sensing the tone of my voice she immediately began to embellish her story. Well, the cottage had been left in a very unsatisfactory state; the place was filthy, untidy, the toilet was filthy and had not been flushed; the floors were disgusting and the rugs were very dirty. I asked her why she hadn't followed the instructions in the Booking Conditions and contacted the caretaker when she realised things were not as she would have expected, and shown evidence that the cleaner had not done her job proper-ly, giving the person a chance to put things right? She replied they had tried to clean up the place themselves and after forty minutes had realised the task was hopeless and they had given up. I tried to explain that we had paid good money for a care-taker, cleaner, and gardener. In the event of such neglect of duty both the caretaker, who would then be in a position to verify her account, and myself, should have been made aware of it immediately and allowed to rectify any problems. At this point the lady became quite abusive, threatening legal action if her money was not returned immediately. I explained that without her having followed correct procedure I had no verifi-cation of the truth of what she was saying and therefore could not accept her story against that of the cleaner, who maintained she was doing her job properly. I had already been charged for four hours of cleaning prior to her arrival. Did she have any evidence at all such as photographs of the state of things on arrival? At this the lady became even more abusive, but offered not one shred of evidence to support her account of things.

Eventually I returned to her the amount she was legally entitled to in such circumstances – the cost of one night's stay in a
chambre d'hôte. We felt by her attitude and the way she changed
and embroidered her story that a most probable explanation
was that they felt the cottage was rather large for the two of
them and too isolated. The other houses in the hamlet were
probably deserted at that time of the year, so they thought
they'd move to a cosier residence and claim their money back
at the same time. However, being five hundred miles away and
not in possession of the full facts made us feel vulnerable and
we found the situation distressing. It was the first particularly
promising season and we were off to an extremely poor start.

The recent happenings had prompted Veronica to write us
vividly elaborate accounts speculating over possible explana-
tions of what might or might not have happened at the *gîte*.
This served only to plunge her into a deep depression – con-
trolled only by 'happy pills' as she described them – which left
untreated would undermine her self-confidence and affect her
ability to make decisions. The episodes left her merely a shadow of the ultra-intelligent, jovial person we had come to rely
on, and would result in sudden unexpected bursts of activity,
over-conscientiousness, and panic over-reactions to casual
comments. At the sight of a family of six staying at the cottage
she would panic and have the *fosse* emptied well before the allotted time 'just to be safe', and warn the visitors not to flush the
loo too often. She would take workmen to the house with visitors still present to discuss routine maintenance work, and this
would inevitably lead to some casual comment on the visitor's
behalf being instantly acted upon. Then the bills kept arriving,
monthly at first, then fortnightly, then weekly, and our money
kept on flowing until there was no more to flow. If we discussed
some topic on the phone and arrived at a certain conclusion, a
letter would later be forthcoming bringing up the same topic as
though we hadn't had the conversation. A bill would arrive, a
covering cheque would be sent, then a further letter would
arrive with more bills requesting me to state what the previous

cheque was meant to cover.

The guests on the other hand, quite enjoyed the extra attention. A few embraced the opportunity to search for something to complain about. One or two were resentful and felt they were being checked up on, others were occasionally privileged to be invited over to Veronica's house for a drink before being chauffeured to the local *pineau* distillery for a tasting session. Some were model guests and fastidious to the extreme, doing more than was expected of them. On the whole the guests were happy, conscientious and considerate people who enjoyed themselves enormously.

The exception to the rule was an odious little man and his family who poured fat down the sink, blocking up the outlet to the garden soak-away. He later insisted on being compensated for the inconvenience and discomfort of having to give up time from his holiday waiting for the plumber to repair the fault. Furthermore he was then unable to allow his children access to the garden because the plumber had dug a third of a metre square hole in the flower bed to try unsuccessfully (according to his account) to unblock the pipe from the outside. In fact the ubiquitous Veronica was to be congratulated for her prompt attention and accomplishing a call-out on a Sunday morning. She later confirmed that the plumber had arrived at 10.30 in the morning, the family had just arisen and although she offered to stay they had assured her they were not going out. If, as he claimed, the plumber was unable to rectify the fault then I had paid a substantial plumber's bill for nothing, and the plumber had misled me on the invoice. I remember feeling at the time that any person who could pursue a case for compensation with such zest and ingenuity could easily have engineered a childproof remedy to the dangers he spoke of. The same family had left the garage two thirds full of bags of refuse depleting our entire stock of refuse bags. They had broken the garden seat yet again and left the cottage in such turmoil it took the cleaner an entire five hours of cleaning and scrubbing to return it to an acceptable state of normality.

Viewing different aspects of and dealing with diverse members of the public are all part and parcel of owning a property in France if it is to be partially self-financing. It can be pleasant and satisfying but all too often obtuse remarks and unappreciative behaviour can lead to disappointment and dismay when you find yourselves at the end of a supposedly 'successful' season – broke. The extra journeys, mileage and time had to be paid for, even the extra journeys involved when a visitor accidentally locked himself out, as happened one day, added to the expense account.

Diversion of the washing-machine outlet away from the *fosse* had not proved to be the complete answer to the problems; the *fosse* had been emptied six times during the season and the emergency reserve fund was being topped up with unparalleled frequency. We decided therefore that providing the criteria could be met, we'd have the second *fosse* installed the following spring as soon as our finances had had time to recover and we could have the procedure explained to us on site. We wrote to Veronica again expressing our concerns over the internal opening of the *fosse*. She phoned Monsieur Jaubert, the *maçon*, reassured us that all would be fine and she would be sending his *devis* for us to sign. The said quote arrived with unbelievable efficiency a few days later, and with equally accustomed efficiency on our part we returned the signed document. One could imagine how surprised we were, when at the beginning of October, just two weeks later, the phone rang. It was a jubilant Veronica.

"I've got some really good news – your *fosse* is finished!"

CHAPTER FIVE

SUNSHINE AND SHOWERS

"Well, after all the trouble I've gone to – you might just say you're pleased," she continued. "He had to go ahead and do the work while the excavator was available, but the weather's been so awful he kept having to stop. I threatened him with everything I could think of if he didn't finish the work before your visitors arrived. I really made him work for his money so I hope you'll say what a good job he's made of it and how pleased you are with it when you send him the money."

I was totally speechless, but she continued in renewed euphoria.

"He's made a new *puits perdu* around the *fosse* and filled it with stones; it was the cheapest option. By the way he said nothing could be done about the interior opening; it has to stay. But isn't it great that you have the increased capacity?"

"Great!" I echoed. I was totally lost for words. A rushed job too!

We wrote to Monsieur Jaubert, asking if it were possible for the internal opening of the *fosse* now to be sealed and clearances to be effected through the external opening only, which had been one of the two essential criteria for going ahead with the work. He explained that only liquid effluent could pass through the link pipe between the two *fosses*, so solid effluent disposal had to be accomplished via the internal opening and liquids via the external opening. Even more perverse was later learning that should we have the misfortune to suffer a further *inundation* it would occur at the site of the internal opening as the *fosse* opening externally was situated at a higher level.

It was impossible to be angry with Veronica. She had made a decision on our behalf, dealt with the situation in her own inimitable way and believed in the circumstances she was

61

acting in our best interest. The truth was we could no longer afford to have someone managing our affairs at a distance, taking decisions for us, and negotiating workers on our behalf. These were tasks we should be doing ourselves. We had to take more responsibility upon ourselves and cut out that middle person. Veronica's letters were becoming lengthy repetitive epistles, almost apologetic at the frequency and size of her bills, yet at the same time charged with gratuitous sarcasm. ("I know it is difficult for you to accept that everything from perfect cleanliness to full equipment remains as you left it four months ago but..."). The tone depicted increasing dissatisfaction, being unable to equate what she considered her miniscule charges with the actual amount of time she was spending coping with a tangled situation she had often helped create initially. She found it more and more difficult to cope with the stress of decision-making and felt that the commission earned plus the expenses received were not commensurate with the ultimate agony of involvement. A chance comment would be taken as personal criticism. I was accused of being too pedantic in my bookkeeping, yet she admitted at the same time that she was lost in her paperwork and trusted my integrity completely. However I failed to convince her that this would be my only reference if mistakes were made. She truly believed we were making vast profits from letting the property for a few weeks, and was astonished when we sent her a copy of the accounts with a typical unfavourable imbalance.

To this day however, I still maintain a great affection for the intelligent, amusing, bizarre Veronica.

That autumn we recalled the words of a client of ours who had made an earlier business trip to the Charente-Maritime. His negotiations had been unsuccessful but he had been introduced to an English couple he described as very helpful, the wife in particular was 'very switched on'. If we ever found we needed caretakers he could thoroughly recommend them. The husband was a builder; the wife spoke fluent French. We decided on the off-chance to give them a ring.

Ros and Neville Saunders had been resident in France for five years. Although Neville was a builder by trade he could turn his hand to most things; he was quite happy to undertake the odd bit of plumbing and electrical work. Ros had done caretaker jobs for other English families and seemed willing to lend a hand where needed, including laundry and gardening. To have a husband and wife caretaker team seemed ideal and so much simpler than wasting time and money chasing up cleaners, gardeners, plumbers and a caretaker who was absent for half the year. We therefore arranged to meet on our next visit in a couple of weeks' time. In the meantime, they would drive past the house and note down a few points.

Two weeks later we sat down to lunch together at the cottage. Ros was nothing approaching the person I'd envisaged during our telephone conversations. She was a tiny, frail looking, woman in her mid-forties who appeared slightly uneasy and apprehensive, and spoke very little during lunch. Neville, who preferred to stand while everyone sat and sipped glasses of *pineau,* could only be persuaded to sit down during lunch. Ironically when later obliged to seat his lightweight frame briefly on the edge of the toilet seat to examine the mains water tap sited next to the toilet, there was a loud crack and much to our amusement, a split appeared across the rim of the toilet. Ros looked mortified.

They loved the *gîte,* comparing it favourably with the state of their own house in the process of being renovated. They seemed very keen to take on the task of caretakers. Their enthusiasm didn't waver when told of the various idiosyncrasies of the place, which seemed a good sign. Their house was about fifteen minutes away by car, so the journey was straightforward. I recall mentioning that I'd love to see the work being done on their own house; I was fascinated seeing other people's ideas come to fruition. Ros seemed a little startled at the idea and I immediately wished I hadn't been quite so forward inviting myself to take a look at their house. Suddenly she smiled and relaxed a little.

"Any time – just give us a ring."

Ros mentioned that the extra work involved opening up for us after the winter break was no problem to her; she would do anything that was needed – painting, laundry, cleaning windows, washing paintwork, even pruning roses. I mentioned the restrictions in farming out work to others and she was adamant that everything that needed doing connected with general household maintenance they were willing to do themselves as a family. I assured her that many of the tasks, such as arranging the *fosse* clearance, I would be able to do myself, the latter by vaguely calculating the average number of flushes per person per day. I could thereby estimate clearance time in the number of weeks' usage, but in the event of over-use by a large family for instance, she might have to bring forward the clearance date and inform me. I would supply instructions, directions and a key for the visitors, and arrange security deposits. It would be appreciated if she could pay the guests a visit, but that was up to her. She opted for allowing guests to get in touch with her if they had any queries but did not volunteer to pay them a visit during their stay, which surprised me somewhat, but I had offered her the choice. One thing I was insistent upon; there would be a mutually agreed contract that spelt out who was responsible for what, crucially so no-one would be in any doubt what their particular responsibilities entailed and there would be no grey areas of overlapping responsibilities. Provision would be made that would allow either party to terminate the contract at the end of a season if they so desired.

We explained that as soon as we had recovered from the expenditure on the new *fosse*, which had happened somewhat prematurely, there were still three major jobs to be completed before we would allow more guests to stay at the *gîte*. We would like the downstairs bedroom carpet ripped up, the floor tiled and the two outside walls plaster-boarded on the inside. The concrete floor of the *salle d'eau* was wet beneath the linoleum; it needed to be replaced with floor tiles. The final task was changing the garage doors, which were in a poor state. Neville explained that if we could choose the tiles he would be very happy to undertake the floors and the plaster-boarding. The local carpenters would give us quotes on the garage doors, as they would have to be specially constructed. We were more than happy with these arrangements; it was all so straightforward, so free of trauma.

The whole community it seemed was in possession of intimate knowledge of our eccentric *fosse* arrangements. No one needed to impart knowledge of the whereabouts of the two openings to the various drivers who pulled up their tanker lorries beside the garage door to perform the all too frequent *vidanges*. They were all discerningly well-informed and undertook their unenviable task in a most business-like fashion, with not a trace of mirth visible at our eccentric arrangement. The excavations involved in sinking the new tank had deposited large amounts of mud over the no longer toothpaste-white and glittering side wall of the cottage, grime that only a power water-jet could be called upon to remove. The capacity had increased from 4,000 litres to 10,000 litres, and we were now only duty-bound to trouble the occupants every eight weeks, on rough calculation of number of flushes per occupant, instead of every three weeks!

Our intentions too, of reducing the amount of weeding necessary by covering the garden beds with wood bark were severely put to the test when we found that an army of moles had invaded the garden. Humps of mud each about twenty-five centimetres in diameter covered the garden beds, scattering the wood bark and inviting the return of the dreaded weeds. The lawn was dotted with similar humps of mud, too numerous to ignore. Although Tilly had her own answer to the problem her amusing 'jumps on the bumps' served only as a temporary exercise as the humps returned as speedily as they could be flattened.

Le Petit Hameau had taken on a new look when the French couple who had moved into the old lady's house decided to mark out the edge of their land by placing large rocks along the border and planting shrubs along the inside of the rocks. This indicated to all that the 'strolling green' was no longer for common use by residents of the hamlet. The pretty stone *moulin* had been removed and the pile of rocks on which it had stood put to use elsewhere. The central garden seat beneath the tree had also disappeared, and the normally immaculate 'green' looked neglected and unkempt, as the grass grew persistently amongst the newly laid stones and shrubs. To provide the necessary stones to mark out their land the stone shack, which belonged to the young French couple, and didn't look in the least appealing even on a sunny day, had been demolished. This presented us with an additional problem and an untimely feeling that our privacy had been invaded. The rear wall of the shack formed part of our garden boundary wall. Its disappearance had left us with an enormous three-metre gap in our boundary wall and an unabated view of Tom and Annabel's barn. Large stones still lay scattered over the area upon which the shack had stood. Believing the scattered stones were all part and parcel of our rights to a boundary wall and had been left with our needs in mind, we carefully but self-consciously lifted the heavy stones across and carefully attempted to rebuild the stone wall. Two exhausting hours later we had achieved something of a crude replacement for the missing boundary wall. Afterwards it occurred to us that it was probably the French couple's duty by law to provide us with the boundary wall of which had been deprived. They had probably left the stones there so *'les pauvres'* English would rush into something it was their legal duty to provide for us. We'd relieved them of the unenviable backbreaking work and for that they appeared more than grateful.

By April the following spring Neville had begun the task of transforming the floor of the shower room. Water was found to be leaking from a pipe beneath the bidet. This Neville quickly fixed and the dampness instantly improved. At the same time he moved the washing-machine socket inside the room to solve the problem of trailing leads into the downstairs bedroom. The dutifully efficient Ros sent photographs of the finished floor; the pink-beige tiles splendidly imparting a soft, clinical glow to the room, which was very encouraging.

One month later he began removing the carpet in the down-stairs bedroom, a fiendish task to undertake as we recollected it had been exceptionally well stuck down. One morning we received a call from Neville. He had discovered a large crack in the cement floor, two centimetres in width, running the full length of the bedroom, with further minor cracks running off the main one at the far end of the room. He thought the move-ment had stabilised and he might just be able to fill the crack and lay the tiles without further widening of the gap, but if it hadn't, we'd risk cracks forming in the new tiles. The alterna-tive was to screed the whole floor, placing a grid over the floor to stabilise it, a more costly option. It was always prudent to play safe so we decided upon the latter, although it would put the schedule back about two weeks. As it happened it was almost two months before the room was finished because Neville had the misfortune to fall off a ladder and bruise his ribs. More photographs arrived of the amazing floor crack and the screed being laid. Not only were we kept up to date with photographic proof that the work had been done, a refreshing-ly kind gesture, but every item of work was carefully moni-tored and recorded with dates, time spent, work completed and amount owed in neat hand-writing. By the time we returned to the Charente in late May the work was not only complete, but the rooms looked absolutely beautiful, with no trace of the pungent dampness in either room. The large glossy blue, beige and cream Italian tiles contributed a luxurious atmosphere to the whole bedroom and blended in so beauti-fully with the colour scheme it looked like an entirely different room. They had done a splendid job.

We'd had luck too, seeking replacements under the guaran-tee, of the kitchen cupboard doors. We returned the doors to the manufacturer in the UK. They agreed the warping should not have happened, and they replaced them without a single question being asked, although we volunteered the circumstances. Apart from the inconvenience of taking up space in the car boot over two journeys, it was a satisfactory outcome. Our new routine of leaving the doors open whenever the opportunity arose seemed to be working. The fault did not re-occur.

That year we had an extended holiday at the cottage, enjoying a balanced mix of days on the beach, sightseeing and jobs around the house. Sunflowers had been planted for the first time in the field opposite the house and a carpet of yellow flowers in full bloom greeted our arrival there. The day after we arrived we were due to collect my sister from the airport at Bordeaux. After a quick lunch we set off for the airport. Just minutes down the road my husband asked what time the plane was due to land. I stared at my watch mesmerised, as a ghastly realisation dawned. The plane had already landed. We had forgotten to put our watches forward by one hour to coincide with French time. We were fifty minutes from the airport. My sister would arrive at a foreign airport, unable to make herself understood, with no one to meet her. We began to panic. We were not on the phone; the only emergency contact she'd been given was Ros and Neville's telephone number. Somehow we must try to get a message through to them that should she try to contact them they should inform her that we were on our way and to stay where she was. We managed to pull off the motorway at a service station and ring Ros and Neville, who seemed hilariously amused by this not unprecedented mistake. The detour added vital minutes on to our journey. At Bordeaux there were further delays, with the main airport road being totally congested with traffic, and we eventually arrived, worried and flustered, two hours late. Where on earth would we look for her? We needn't have worried. We spotted her almost immediately by the exit doors, seated on an empty trolley absorbed in her book, having rung Ros and Neville and been fully reassured that we were on our way. Once again Ros and Neville had saved the day and she was able to enjoy her stay with us. In particular she enjoyed the splendidly cheap

Sunflowers had been planted for the first time in the field opposite the house and a carpet of yellow flowers in full bloom greeted our arrival there.

local wine, and the eventual advent of incoherence as each evening faded into a regular pattern of slow intoxication. Her companions did not have the heart to tell her that her sighting of the frightened little field mouse scuttling across the floor from the patio door to the sanctuary of her bedroom was not an hallucination!

One stiflingly hot afternoon we decided to pay Ros and Neville a visit, perhaps even acquire some interesting tips and ideas on restoring old buildings that might be put to future use. The directions were difficult to follow and several telephone calls later we spotted Rob, their younger son, who was a year older than Tilly, waving and indicating us into a narrow lane which led us towards the house. We had not chosen a good time, as they'd had unexpected visitors that afternoon in the form of Ros's ex-husband, who with his girl friend had called to see his son, the elder boy Mark, who was nineteen. Everyone was gathered on bench seats around a long trestle table, attempting to combat the excessive heat by emptying glasses of ice-cool orange juice mixed with refreshing lemonade. We had decided it was not a good time and we shouldn't stay but immediately we were introduced to the visitors, hurriedly made welcome and joined the party for what was intended to be a brief chat. Rob and Tilly played with the dog, Tilly being most amused when Rob threw a ball into a large dense bush and the dog leapt in after it, completely disappearing for a brief moment. The animal then reappeared with the ball in its mouth, and rushed back for the process to begin again. Mark had dismissed his father's company, preferring instead to watch videos inside the house to the rare and apparently unwelcome visit by his blood relative, and an hour later they left without really seeing him.

Two hours later our intended half-hour visit was about to encroach upon the evening hours when Neville suddenly stood up and announced he'd like to show us round the house. Ros didn't wish to accompany the tour and remained in the kitchen to prepare dinner. After trudging through a cool but dingy *salon*, through the cluttered kitchen and up the stairs leading to a small double bedroom with a large mosquito net surrounding the double bed, there was little else left to see. We clambered through a hole into the roof space, where a small section had been divided off to form a bedroom for Rob. Neville was full of plans and knew exactly what he intended to build in the roof space. We crossed to the other side, climbed a ladder into an enormous area large enough to build half a dozen rooms ensuite. I wondered how they managed to avoid the open spaces and keep warm in the winter. Neville explained that when they bought the house the roof space was full of wood, enough for him to complete the entire work envisaged necessary. He'd been quite excited at the prospect, for in French law the house is purchased as seen unless otherwise indicated in writing. No such stipulations were recorded in the agreement and Neville had been assured that all the contents including the wood would be included in the purchase price. When they came to take possession the house had been totally stripped bare, and finding themselves trapped by the language barrier they had been unable to make proper negotiation and found there was nothing they could do about it. Five years on with substantial knowledge of the language things might have been very different. I had the oddest feeling that Ros did not share Neville's dream. I found her still in the kitchen. She seemed embarrassed at being seen amidst the turmoil of her own surroundings, but relieved that I still wanted them to look after the cottage.

The afternoon highlighted for us the problems of gullible families settling in France with basic knowledge of the language, with enticing but sketchy ideas of how they would manage financially, but unable to channel ideas for fulfilling their dreams of restoring a property into realistic possibilities. Neville had the expertise, but had fallen into the trap of having no independent income, therefore being forced to find full time work to provide for the family, watching other peoples' dreams grow, while chance allowed him little time to do renovation on

71

his own property. His ideas could only remain fantasies.

One afternoon, after all our visitors had left, Tilly was out horse riding with friends staying at a neighbouring *gîte*. We propped the ladder against the side wall of the cottage and picked up the roller to see just how far we could reach up the large blank wall, which was beginning to look decidedly shabby. Surprisingly Keith could just about reach the highest point between the front and back roofs and he daubed the end of the roller into the paint, to prove a point. By the time Tilly returned from her afternoon activities we had between us, quite remarkably, completed painting the whole of the side wall, a fairly substantial area, returning the wall to the smart dazzling toothpaste-white it was always intended to be. Encouraged by our success the following day we decided to make Monsieur Gauthier's day by painting the outside of the tiny wooden shutters upstairs and the metal shutters downstairs a delicate shade of pale blue. The transformation was astonishing. The cottage definitely had the beginnings of the picture-postcard look. Or so it appeared to our somewhat biased minds.

So inspired were we by the effectiveness of the earlier outside painting, we decided in the autumn to finish the job. The front of the cottage encompassed a smaller square footage than the side but painting could not be accomplished by the easier method of using a roller. The surface was extremely uneven and the wall height became shorter towards the right as the cottage was built on a slope. In areas that had been surfaced in the past, this had partially crumbled away leaving bare stone and cement. Any attempt at resurfacing would alter the character of the cottage and it would lose its individuality. Cracks and hollowed out areas between the stones had to be re-cemented, attempting to avoid condemning to an expeditious death any poor obdurate lizard who happened to have found a primitive home there. We toiled all day and well into the evening using medium sized paint brushes to cover the areas between the stones. It seemed to take forever. Fate however was on our side. The following day fierce winds blew in from the estuary. That was the day the farmers chose to plough the field opposite the cottage, sending dense clouds of fine dust billowing towards the front of the cottage with what could have been disastrous consequences, had it happened a day earlier.

All that remained of the major jobs was the garage door replacement. As anyone knows who has tried to get anything done quickly in France the Wheels of Fortune move very slowly indeed. It is said that the typical French workman never likes to say *"non"* and disappoint anyone, so inevitably he says *"oui"* to everything then keeps the person hanging in suspense and fails to turn up on the allotted commencement date. He does not mean to let you down, it is part of the French culture that nothing ever seems to happen to order. If one can accept the fact that there is no such thing as a deadline in France, and accept that a job will be done eventually, it avoids much of the frustration. A *devis*, promised in April for instance, can be expected to arrive in October. The garage doors were replaced almost exactly a year after the carpenter was first approached and agreed to do the work. Made from *bois exotique* the two coats of stain/preservative we put on after the doors were hung gave the doors the final finishing touch. Although expensive, they looked so beautiful it was money well spent. At least we no longer held out a hand of welcome to each and every one of our rodent cousins who needed a winter refuge. It was unfortunate that Neville had conveyed the idea to the carpenter that the garage was never likely to be used for a car. The carpenter had as a direct consequence of this made the garage door threshold of aluminium which would not take the weight of a car. Occasionally visitors liked to back the rear of their vehicles into the garage to load up the car boot. We were rather surprised to find the rejected garage doors still lying inside the garage but we did learn that workmen would not normally take old parts away unless specifically asked to do so, rather like the custom of the post-box. I gather that it is illegal in France for a postman to enter the gate of a property to deliver mail; the post-box has to be located at or by the garden gate.

Only a fool believes that when the last major task is finished you can sit down, relax and enjoy yourself for a while. A new concern had arisen. A fine crack had appeared in the plasterboard above the inside of the kitchen door, and outside the large wedge-shaped stone directly above the kitchen door shutters had a small crack running obliquely along the cement parallel to the edge of the stone. The kitchen door, which opened inwards, was becoming a little difficult to open. The lower edge of the door was dropping slightly on the door-handle side, gouging a deep groove in the linoleum. It was something we needed to keep an eye on and take professional advice about if it got any worse. Neville agreed to keep an eye on it; he decided there had been some movement but thought it was nothing to worry about.

There was some cause for celebration. Tom and Annabel had their swimming pool at last, and by way of celebrating, had gone out and spent 2000 francs on a variety of saplings which they intended to plant around the area beyond the pool to provide patches of shade for sunbathers. They had bought black plastic bin-liners to stretch across the base of the trees to protect the delicate root systems until they became established. The pool itself was completely hidden from the lane by a substantial hedge, affording them complete privacy from tractors, passing vehicles and the like.

The new owners of the big house were beginning to establish themselves, with lots of renovation work going on there – a team of workmen hard at it all day long with drills, saws and hammers. One day the wife, who introduced herself as Audrey, invited us over to see the work they had done. A dazzling new swimming pool could be seen from the elegant triple French windows of the lounge. The upper floor of the house had in the space of eighteen months been completely renovated. I counted at least eight new bedrooms, each with *en suite* shower rooms, toilets and wash basins. There had been no expense spared and the result looked extremely impressive. Audrey told us they intended inviting some of her husband's American friends over the following summer. She had spent a lot of time at the house, overseeing the work, and was pleased with the outcome. We were totally in awe of the spectacular appearance of the upper floor restoration work. We could see beneath the quietly spoken, gentle and kindly manner, that this was a lady who possessed a sagacious eye for business. She told us how one middle-aged gentleman perceiving money was no object had been so greedy he'd priced himself out of the job in spite of his impressive qualifications. Her words again brought to mind that earlier incident and the sudden departure of the man in question. We congratulated her on the enormous amount of work that had been achieved in such a short time, and returned the compliment by inviting her to take a quick look at our cottage. That exercise took all of five minutes and hardly matched the half hour grand tour of *la grande maison blanche*!

The unusually harsh winter of 1996 was for many the worst in living memory. For three days most of the motorways of France were impassable and the whole of France was virtually at a standstill. In Charente-Maritime temperatures of minus 13 degrees were recorded and during the worst days people did not move either to or from their homes until it was safe to do so. Fortunately for us Neville had anticipated problems, had been over to the house and emptied the toilet cistern and all the taps. There were many stories circulating of people who had returned to their homes and found burst pipes and thousands of francs' worth of damage. Tom and Annabel had lost every one of their lovely saplings, and we had lost the beautiful mimosa that had graced the bottom of our garden each winter with spectacular sweeping sprays of fluffy golden flowers and grey-green feathery leaves. It had been much admired by passers-by who reckoned a single spray of this most perfect of specimens would have fetched 50 francs in the weekly market at Gémozac! The tall umbrella pine, that stood at the head of and harboured the delicate plants in the stone trough, protecting them from the blistering heat of the summer sun, stood brittle and brown. A whole row of tall conifers standing in splendid isolation, originally planted to act as a windshield for the house on the hill two kilometres up the lane, had also succumbed to the hard winter frost. The house at the back of the hamlet occupied by the French couple was displaying an intimidating and ungainly seven centimetre wide crack down the outside wall extending from the upper floor shutters down to ground level. The owners seemingly unconcerned were exhibiting a typical French indifference to the catastrophe.

A family we had met earlier and with whom we had become friends, who owned a house situated in the middle of a field with acres of surrounding land, just beyond the next village, visited their house at Easter with the express purpose of finishing off their new bathroom. Instead they were obliged to spend their valuable time doing emergency repairs when they found a friendly owl, who had taken possession of their roof space, had nibbled through the insulation causing burst water pipes. Consequently the ceiling had collapsed, leaving a pile of rubble in their living room.

A strange anomaly awaited us on our visit in May. It appeared Neville had removed the front of the water heater for some reason. Although we had been warned that the taps had been emptied, we turned on the mains having checked all the taps were turned off, to witness water cascading out of the pipe in the water heater. Water sprayed over the wall, the contents of the kitchen bench and any person within a one and a half metre radius of the source. There seemed to be no means of halting the flow other than at the mains, which effectively meant we had no water, in particular hot water. We noticed also that the garage door had been left unlocked. We phoned Neville and Ros and within fifteen minutes a furious Ros had appeared with Mark. She told us that Neville had been offered a lift to England and had rushed off at short notice leaving them entirely in the lurch. She had no idea what was going on with the water heater but knew Neville had checked the place over just before the frosts arrived, and suggested Mark should take a look at it. In the meantime Tom had examined the apparatus and managed to stem the flow of water. Mark who seemed a shy boy and rarely spoke, perhaps because he now spoke mainly French, did a silent survey of the water heater, tampered with a few screws, announced its recovery from the affliction, and that the heater could be put back into use. We thanked them for rushing to our aid and relaxed for a while over coffee and biscuits.

During our short visit we once or twice convinced ourselves that we could smell gas but put it down to the apparatus having been dowsed with water and having not been used for a while. We were concerned also that the crack above the kitchen door had apparently widened a little, and the door was quite stiff to open. We called round to see Monsieur Jaubert, the local *maçon* who had installed the subsidiary *fosse*, to ask if he would take a look at it. On an earlier occasion, Annabel had called there to inquire about fixing a hole in her roof, and was astonished to find the whole family from grandmother to small grandchild, seated round a huge kitchen table making sausages. On this occasion he was not at home and we left a message with his wife. Surprisingly he turned up at dawn the following morning to inspect the movement in the wall. After taking a brief look inside and out he announced it was absolutely nothing to worry about. In the summer he explained, the gap would look wider but in the cool wet weather it would close up again. We explained that the door was sticking badly, but he shook his head dismissively. His answer to the problem was *"coupez la porte au dessous."* We weren't convinced that enabling the door to open in this way while watching a growing gap develop at the top of the door was the advice we sought, and with a reasonably full summer season ahead of us we did not exactly feel reassured.

The bitterly cold winter was followed uncharacteristically by an unusually stifling hot summer, when temperatures soared to 40 degrees, plants wilted and died through lack of moisture and the grass remained brown throughout the summer. Far from the trouble-free summer we longed for, the new washing machine broke down just days out of warranty. Ros also broke the news that there had been substantial damage to the new garage door. In spite of being warned that the garage was for storage use only, a family appeared to have backed a heavy vehicle into the garage, flattening the aluminium threshold, preventing the garage door from being closed properly and the key could no longer be located in the lock. To make matters worse the family involved denied they had caused any damage whatsoever to the garage doors, even to the point of claiming they were unable to unlock the garage door when they arrived and the damage had obviously been caused by previous visitors. The fact that this hadn't been reported either at the time or later to us, rather threw their story out of the window, but the family continued to maintain they were not responsible in any way for the damage, something we found rather unnerving.

One family cracked one of the window panels from corner to corner, and Ros sent us a neat little bill for 100 francs to cover the cost of the glass and replacement, which seemed very reasonable. Before writing to the family concerned, I phoned Ros to make sure the damage had been done by the visitors, as we knew there were three panes that were slightly cracked. Yes, she was certain this was new damage, as she always opened all the windows while cleaning the cottage and the damaged pane was just above the window opening and very distinct. Again the damage to the window was fiercely and categorically denied by the family concerned and I had the unenviable task of writing to the family enclosing copies of the bill for the damaged goods and the caretaker's report.

I was beginning to believe I hadn't the stomach for it all, but I'm told that very few people actually admit to damage or breakage. Such things were generally discovered by accident, as in my case when I spotted a dead wasp lying at the base of a glass light globe in the toilet cubicle. I reached up to unscrew the globe to clean it, and noticed the globe had been sheered off at its neck and the broken piece balanced on the light bulb, but only after I'd cut my hand on the jagged edge. I was reminded of an incident Veronica related to us once. She was dutifully inspecting a house prior to some tenants' departure and noticed that each time she went to inspect the toilet there was someone occupying it. Finally she gave up trying. Everything appeared in order and she handed back the security deposit. Too late she found out the loo seat had been broken and lay in two jagged pieces balanced on the rim of the toilet!

There had been numerous complaints about the gas, ranging from 'a slight smell of gas', to 'a strong smell of gas permeating throughout cottage', to 'a nauseating smell of gas that one was permanently aware of.' Ros told us the engineer had been to look at it and had found that someone had left the washer off the gas cylinder and it had now been fixed. She had written a note in the visitor's book to that effect. It was disconcerting therefore when people still complained about a smell of gas, though Ros continued to reassure us that it seemed all right and people were most probably reading the visitors' book and imagining the gas smell still to be present. There was always a slight smell of gas from cylinder gas, she insisted, and it would be more evident when a place was closed up even for a few hours. Our reports with receipts for gas cylinders attached however, told a different story. A gas cylinder was reputed to last an average family from six to eight weeks. We were being charged for cylinders of gas at a rate of two per week. An awful lot of gas must have been escaping. I asked Ros if she could persuade the gas engineer to have another look at it.

One day a follow-up phone call revealed the unexpected news that Neville was in hospital in Bordeaux having suffered a heart attack. The family did not seem in any way concerned and reassured us he was recovering and would be coming home soon. Apart from someone trying to plug the iron into the socket of the standard lamp, which operated from the room's main light switch, turned off at the time, things were fine at the cottage. Instead of trying the iron in another socket the visitor had phoned Ros complaining the iron wasn't working. I was surprised Ros could mention such trivial things with her husband ill in hospital. It was his own fault, she claimed, he drank too much and smoked too much.

A short time after this conversation, one morning out of the blue, there came a phone call from a lady who introduced herself as Ros's mum. She was calling from the north of England. Ros had asked her to phone to let us know that she had left Neville and could be contacted at a friend's house in the next but one village to ours in France. She gave us the friend's telephone number and said Ros would write and fill us in with the details. Staggered by the news, we wondered what on earth had happened, and so soon after Neville's heart attack.

CHAPTER SIX

IRREGULARITIES

Ros very soon made contact. She was anxious to reassure us in her letter that everything was under control at the *gîte*. She made very little reference to the split or indeed to her personal circumstances, apart from indicating that Neville had taken the car and gone to England so her friend was being very kind and ferrying her around in her car. The garage door lock at the cottage had been fixed, the threshold straightened and reinforced, and the doors taken off and realigned. I asked about the bill for the washing machine repair, but she said she hadn't yet had the bill. She even managed to joke that someone had complained the lawn was the wrong shade of green! Some visitors, six adults, had arrived early, dumped their bags and six suitcases in the *salon* and lay on the lawn sunbathing. Ros had indicated that they weren't meant to be there until 4 o'clock and would therefore need to move their belongings for her to clean the cottage. They refused to move anything and she couldn't therefore clean the lounge floor. The party subsequently complained that the floors were dirty on arrival. A large hole had appeared in front of the new *fosse,* where a lorry carrying sand and gravel to the house behind ours had backed over it. She promised to deal with it.

Her next letter was equally nonchalant. She and the boys had moved out of her friend's house as her friend had relatives staying and the house was too small for them all. She had moved back to her own house for a while, and had managed to sell it to an English couple. Unfortunately Neville had returned from England unexpectedly as a result of which both she and Mark had ended up in hospital in plaster casts. Mark had a badly broken nose and she had torn ligaments in her arm. A new address appeared at the top of her letter; she and her younger son were now living in a refuge. Her elder son was living at her friend's house as he was no longer considered a minor and therefore could not stay at the refuge with her. She hoped that when the sale of the house was finalised, they would be able to move into a flat so the three of them could live under the same roof again. She asked, as the summer season was ending, if things got really desperate, she might move into the cottage for a short while, just at weekends, so she and the boys could be together occasionally. Of course it would be all right, I told her, providing we came to some implicit arrangement over fuel cost. A neighbour was much more explicit in her exhortation; she thought it would be a mistake to become involved in marital matters and believed the relationship between Ros and ourselves should be kept strictly on a business level. However, I felt it was impossible and quite heartless to turn one's back on a person in such difficult circumstances.

Ros's letter was the first indication on her part that the separation was permanent. It was the first reference to any violence having taken place. We felt desperately sorry for her in her awful predicament. At the same time we found it difficult to believe that the jovial, amusing Neville we thought we knew, was capable of violence. There had been not the slightest hint on her part that her life was falling apart, although she'd never had very much to say in his company. She told me she was trying to retrieve as many of her belongings from the house as she could, and as quickly as she could, because Neville was selling many of her belongings, and burning the rest. She had put a couple of boxes of belongings in our garage. She hoped it was all right to do so; she didn't know what else to do with them. They would be moved as soon as she could manage it. That was perfectly fine, I reassured her. "Just let me know what I can do to help."

One Sunday afternoon in mid-September we received an unexpected telephone call from Neville. He'd just driven past our house in France and he'd seen his stepson Mark and some of his French friends sitting on the patio. He'd stopped and asked what they were doing there. Mark had explained he was living there. Neville felt we should know about it as some of Mark's friends were of very dubious character and he certainly wouldn't want any of them in his house. One had been vomiting in the garden as he'd driven up. We were quite disturbed at the implications of this report and the nature of the telephone call. We decided we must ring Ros and find out what was going on, as according to Neville there had been no sign of her at the house. Her responsibilities as key-holder did not extend to passing the house keys over to her son. Ros was at her friend's house and did not appear surprised at Neville's telephone call. He was simply making mischief, causing her endless problems, following her everywhere, she explained. Mark had dropped off a box of her belongings at the house, and was probably trying to put his stepfather off the scent. Immediately I had visions of a jealously outraged Neville trying to burn down our house containing Ros's belongings. We must try to remain neutral and not get involved in their marital squabbles, I urged my husband. We didn't really know where the actual truth lay. Nevertheless whether we liked it or not, we had become embroiled in the whole messy business.

Keith suddenly came up with the idea that as he had an allocated week off in late September and it was during school time, he would drive down to the cottage alone, take some more small items of furniture and put the time to good use. His intention was to fill the holes in the garage wall, try to make it mouse-proof, then paint the wall. It was a task he'd been intending to tackle for some time. The job was time-consuming. It meant when we visited at half term a month later there would be no all-consuming tasks to be done and we could spend some time enjoying ourselves. At first I was not in favour of the idea. It was a very long journey to make twice in one week without a co-driver, and we were not on the telephone at the cottage. Even the mobile was out of range. In the event of an emergency neither of us could be contacted. We then thought of Tom and Annabel, who did have a phone, and decided that with their permission, I would phone the barn at 23.00 hours each evening. We had a key to the barn and had an arrangement whereby they would open up and air our cottage when they were down at Le Petit Hameau and we would do the same for them. The arrangement worked well. If they ever needed to borrow a drill, a spade or a heater, they could help themselves. Tom and Annabel were fine about the telephone arrangement. So rather reluctantly, burdened with a large carton of food, cool bag filled with casseroles, ham, fruit, vegetables and salads, and a sleeping bag to save time making and unmaking a bed, I waved him goodbye early one morning for his lone journey south, via Dieppe.

At the pre-appointed hour I duly telephoned the barn. The phone just rang and rang. By my crude reckoning he should have arrived at 21.00 hours, allowing extra time for the sea route but taking time off the journey for the shorter drive. At 23.30 I rang again. I was about to put down the phone for the second time when suddenly a familiar, but panting voice answered. The boat it seemed had been an hour late arriving, the journey had taken that much longer and he'd just pulled up in the back lane when he'd heard the telephone ringing in the barn. He'd grabbed the key and the torch and raced to answer it. He'd not yet unpacked, was feeling pretty tired, but all was well.

The following evening it was rather a different story he had to tell. He'd unpacked the car the night before, put the food in the fridge and more or less taken straight to his sleeping bag, but was surprised that the electricity mains was on when he arrived. The following morning he had opened up all the windows and been quite surprised by what had greeted him. There was strange additional furniture all over the house, books, videos, CDs, and clothes lying in every room. The double bed was in the twin-bedded room, and the twin beds were in the double bedroom. Tilly's bicycle was hanging half-way up the garage wall, minus the brand new seat we had recently bought for it. There were car hubs strung up and hanging

decoratively from the beams in the bedrooms and on the bedroom door. Keith had been unable to find his extension lead
and finally had spotted it attached to a hi-fi upstairs. A fair
amount of electricity had been used, the spare gas cylinder was
empty and all the candles had disappeared apart from the
stubs remaining in the candleholders. We'd had every reason
to take Neville's call seriously. It appeared Mark and his
friends had been living at the cottage, yet nothing made sense.
It certainly would have taken more than one person to move
the double bed, and for what purpose other than to make their
own indelible mark on the place, would anyone bother to
move beds around? We were perplexed, and more than a little
alarmed at the weird attributes of these intruders. I couldn't
help thinking that anyone merely wishing to secure a roof over
their head would have behaved a little less intrusively and
with a little respect for the owners' property.

That day Keith telephoned Ros's friend from the village, and
was surprised to hear Mark's voice at the other end of the line.
He asked him if he'd been staying at the *gîte* and a sheepish
voice replied that his mother had said it would be all right. In
an unprecedented outburst Keith replied that he was only in
France for a short time and did not expect to have to clear up
his mess and go around searching for leads and tools. He
should not have been staying at the house on his own, without
his mother and without our knowledge. We had not reached
any arrangement, and he was extremely disappointed by his
unorthodox and inconsiderate behaviour. A few minutes later
Mark's scooter drew up outside the house, and a rather sub-
dued and morose Mark appeared, apologising to Keith and
offering to move the furniture back. As it was by this time, late
in the evening, and Keith was very tired, knowing Mark could
not move the furniture without his help and not having the
strength to perform major upheavals at that time of night, he
declined the offer.

Before the week ended Keith had a visit from Ros. Her friend
dropped her off on the way to pick up her daughter from

school. She wanted to put my husband in the picture as far as Neville was concerned. She had, it seemed, been a battered wife for most of the eighteen years of their marriage. For most of that time she had convinced herself that somehow she was to blame for his violent behaviour, which mostly occurred after bouts of excessive drinking. Lately his violence had extended to beating the children and that was when she decided enough was enough, and had decided to end the marriage, sell the house and seek a divorce. He was an extremely obsessive man, believing that she was his lawful possession, and would not accept her decision. He continually followed her around, spreading rumours about the family, and her in particular.

She had seemed so tragic a figure, so vulnerable, sitting pouring her heart out, Keith hadn't the heart to tell her what Mark had been up to whilst supposedly 'dropping off' a few things for his mother. Acknowledging her plight, he merely informed her that the beds had been changed round, and a few things moved. "Oh! I wonder why he did that?" she asked. She seemed a little confused by it all, promising everything would be put back as it was, and dashed off, as her lady chauffeur had now returned with her daughter.

Filling in holes in the wall proved to be tedious and time consuming, and Keith was determined to finish the task he'd set himself, working all day long and well into the evening to do so. There was just enough time to give the wall a coat of paint and allow himself the luxury of one trip to the beach to breathe the sea air before setting off on his marathon return trip to England.

A minor point he'd forgotten to mention in the wake of the various happenings at the *gîte* was that the badly cracked windowpane had not been replaced as had been indicated earlier. The intervening crises had reduced our priorities to microscopic proportions.

Half term was just five weeks away. Our trip to the Charente was to remain unheralded. Ros was informed only in the last two days prior to our arrival in order to secure the desired element of surprise. This time our worst suspicions were confirmed. We unlocked the kitchen door to find that once again the electricity had been switched on at the mains. The fridge was on and there was milk, cheese and a lone chocolate mousse in the fridge. In the linen basket our duvet covers and sheets were lying folded but damp. Although the beds had been returned to the correct rooms, there was still furniture placed in favoured positions throughout the house, books on the bookshelf, and videos in the bedroom. The gas cylinder was still lying empty, and Tilly could not use her bicycle as the saddle was still missing. In the garden, the large stones had been collected from the herb bed and strewn around the garden, and our pottery vases, ash trays and candle-holders lay on the patio. My head throbbed with fury and confusion that someone could abuse the trust we'd placed in them, but my voice kept echoing "why? – why on earth?"

The next morning I spotted our rear neighbours about to drive off. They had been there a week and were staying another few days. They confirmed that a 'young English lad' and a couple of his French friends had been staying at the cottage, and had left the day before we arrived. My fury was mounting. I turned to Keith. "How could they? After you'd had words with him. He has taken absolutely no notice of your warning." We drove to the village to ring Ros's friend. Mark was conveniently out. We asked if it were possible for us to make contact with Ros but the lady of the house explained that she'd just seen her and would not be seeing her again until the end of the week. We briefly explained why we felt justified in demanding that in the circumstances Mark return the key he was holding within twenty-four hours and return to the cottage only to collect his possessions. He was totally banned from otherwise setting foot in the place. Circumstances, we felt, had affected him in such a manner that his presence could no longer be considered desirable at the *gîte*. She seemed a little taken aback, emphasising that Mark had always been a charming and helpful boy. The 'charming and helpful boy' did not return the key or collect his belongings and it proved an impossible task to track down Ros's whereabouts.

It was obvious to us that Mark had no intention of either paying the money owed to cover the fuel cost, or of returning the brand new saddle to the bike. Mark believed, as his mother had said he could stay there, that she would settle up with us. Ros had completely divorced herself from any responsibility for the money that Mark owed. The fact that both mother and son believed it was not necessary to offer payment of any kind or even an apology for the loss and inconvenience they had placed upon us made us more resolute they should at least determine right from wrong. In our next letter to Ros we sent a bill for the gas and electricity used, a part contribution to the *fosse* payment, and the cost of the replacement saddle we'd had to buy. Strangely, we were never offered any apology for what had happened. Ros's one consuming thought was for her own reputation, thinking that Keith might believe she had been lying when she'd told him Mark was only dropping off boxes of goods at the house.

We returned to the *gîte*, collected up all the furniture and incidentals that were scattered all over the house, put them all together along one side of the garage, and covered them over with dust sheets. Books, clothes, CDs and other items of belongings were put in boxes and bags and stored with the rest. Hopefully by so doing we had eliminated the bizarre but real feeling of permanence attached to the implantation of these belongings. At the same time we were exceedingly aware that these few items were probably sadly all that remained of her life's possessions and small treasures. It was a heart breaking, pitiful sight.

Apart from our squatter problems, a forlorn apparition was upsetting Keith more than anything, that of his newly painted white garage wall, which in the space of five weeks had turned a patchy shade of gold and looked quite foul. He was so bitterly disappointed he could not show off his week's hard work. We speculated as to the cause of the severe discolouring and what remedy would effect an instant cure. Something in the make-up of the stone could have caused it, or simply damp. It was unfortunate that the disdainful Mark and his cigarette puffing friends could not in this instance be blamed for the passive smoking effect on the wall. We tried repainting parts of the wall but within twenty-four hours the wall was again beginning to discolour. A neighbour suggested we paint the rest of the wall a matching gold but the suggestion did not meet with wild enthusiasm. Finally in desperation and not exactly motivated by some veritable scientific theory I decided to give the wall a coat of all-purpose primer. The following day the wall was still white and mysteriously remained white up to the time of our departure.

There was another thrilling piece of news. At the bottom of the garden just in front of where the mimosa had once stood, at least half a dozen baby mimosas had blithely sprung up to take its place. This fine act of nature had engendered tiny nine inch shoots with silken grey-green leaves enhancing this neglected section of the garden and bringing a breath of fresh air amidst the chaos.

In November that year we received a surprise telephone call from Neville. He wanted to know if Ros had passed on an outstanding account of his for the work that he'd carried out on the damaged garage door. We told him Ros had certainly not mentioned any further costs and asked why he had left it so long. In fact we had specifically asked them if there were any other outstanding accounts before writing to the visitors who had caused the damage. He thought Ros had told us about the money, he retorted. He waffled on about the one and a half hours spent doing temporary repairs on the first day, the two hours spent chasing up the carpenter on the second day and a further one and a half hours helping the carpenter straighten out the threshold. We therefore, according to his calculations, owed him five hundred francs. It was extremely difficult when deliberately being baffled with figures, to comprehend over the phone what hours he was attributing to what work. I asked him if he could write to us itemising everything and I would have the work verified. Almost three weeks went by before the letter arrived. It concluded if we could forward the money to his parents' address in England he would accept a cheque for fifty pounds instead of payment in francs. I forwarded a copy of the letter to Ros, asking her to comment on the bill and verify if the work had genuinely and necessarily occurred. In the interim there were more calls from Neville, asking if we had received his letter. I tried to explain that I had written for confirmation, was awaiting a reply and I would be in touch as soon as I'd heard anything. More calls followed. I again explained that as he had waited so long before telling us he had not been paid for the work, he could surely wait a little longer until I'd heard from France. In his final call he spoke to Keith. He emphasised he'd always been straight with us and sensing Keith's cautiousness, seemed keen to unburden himself. Ros was not divorcing him, he insisted, HE was divorcing her. He further insisted he'd never laid a finger on Ros, but she had told so many lies about him. Lying came very easily to her and she could lie very convincingly, he said. On the last occasion, he explained, he had gone to the friend's house to serve the divorce papers and as he was pushing them through the post-box Ros came towards him brandishing a broom-handle. He hadn't attacked her; she had attacked him. When Mark had joined in the affray, he was forced to defend himself, and the boy had come off the worst. He told Keith he'd had a further heart attack; he couldn't work and was desperate for money. If Keith could find it in his heart to send the money he was owed he would be most grateful. Occasionally, the fine line drawn between absolute truth and pure fabrication can be difficult to discern, even for those closely involved, and during conversations can shift wildly and unintentionally between the two with a typically unsettling outcome. Basically we did not know who was telling the truth, but we suspected the truth lay somewhere between the two conflicting accounts. We had never discovered Ros with a single bruise on her, and we could only believe the facts, not other peoples' accounts of the facts.

In her reply to my letter Ros repeated that if she'd believed we'd owed extra money she would have sent a bill at the time. Neville had spent one and a half hours at the house that day, but only because he wouldn't allow her the car, insisting he needed it for himself. He had undertaken to go off and find the carpenter who lived five minutes down the road, while she was cleaning the house; so it was hardly inconvenient. The 'temporary repairs' to the garage door she insisted, referred to his wedging a pick-axe against the door handle to prevent anyone entering. He did spend an hour and a half with the plumber the next day, but to try and charge 500 francs when he only charged 400 francs for a full day's work, was ludicrous, she concluded. We were now placed in the most difficult of positions, walking a fine line through No Man's Land between the battle forces, and desperately trying to steer a path of neutrality. After deliberating the matter carefully we decided he should be paid for the one and a half-hours he spent assisting the carpenter and we sent a cheque in full and final settlement of the claim. At the same time we took the opportunity to inform him that as he was now living in England and had left the address printed on the contract, the contract was now automatically invalid and therefore terminated. The cheque was cashed, and nothing more was heard about the matter, apart from a comment in one of Ros's letters, that Neville had phoned her friend to tell her that we were taking him to court over the matter.

Ros, in the meantime, was determined she would still be able to continue working with us. She would be moving into her own flat in January, be able to carry on as usual, and would have her own means of transport shortly. She intended moving her belongings out of the cottage as soon as her flat was ready. Mark would pay the money he owed us as soon as possible. Everything would be fine.

At last we received the engineer's account for fixing the washing machine, over a year after the work had been done, with apologies from Ros for not having sent it before. It was only when the engineer contacted her wondering why he hadn't been paid that she realised it had been sitting at the bottom of her pile. The invoice was for quite a substantial amount of francs considering it was a new washing machine. I was able to decipher, with help from my French dictionary that the problem had been that the motor had seized due to a faulty connection in the power supply. I didn't wish to apportion blame but it appeared as if the problem had arisen after Neville had resited the power supply, which probably accounted for the embarrassingly late arrival of the bill. I promptly paid the account directly to the engineer, and apologised sincerely for the delay in payment, and nothing further was said about the matter.

It was a very last-minute decision to visit the cottage the following May half term. There was no opportunity to let Ros know of our plans. We were extremely worried about Ros's ability to cope in her present circumstances. Nothing had been done about the replacement window panel, and the gas service was still waiting to be fixed. We could not allow another season of constant complaints about a gas leak and there was a mere two weeks to go before the season commenced. The element of surprise would give us the opportunity to judge for ourselves how well Ros was coping.

The Southwest had suffered weeks of constant rain, including a very wet Easter. We arrived to find the roses in full bloom; they had never looked more gorgeous – that was after the two-metre high grass enveloping them had been cut back to reveal their magnificent blooms. Nettles and grass half covered the garage door; we literally had to hack our way through to open the garage door. We arrived very late at night, and very tired. The next morning the first thing I noticed was that the television was missing, which was somewhat worrying. Tilly opened the patio shutters and gasped, horrified. "Mummy, come and see the garden. You won't believe what it looks like." I groaned. The grass was nearly five feet high, completely smothering the lavender and other shrubs desperate to gain recognition. The rose bed and herb beds were carpeted in a tangled mass of light weeds covering the bark. Keith decided that without changing the oil and renewing the spark plug in the old lawn mower we would not have the slightest chance of reclaiming the garden yet again from the absolute jungle that presented itself. So after a quick breakfast he set about overhauling the lawn mower, while I got to work with the secateurs.

The furniture and various oddments belonging to Ros that had occupied a large area of the garage had been removed at last, but the gas cylinder remained empty and the saddle had not been returned. The hole that had appeared at one side of the *fosse* was still gaping and dangerous. It was certainly large enough for a car tyre to become wedged and was in need of urgent attention. Monsieur Jaubert was reluctantly persuaded to return and fill in the hole, then promptly explained that although the work was guaranteed, we must pay him 100 francs *pour les pierres*!

On this occasion, we felt we must get in touch with Ros and invite her over for a discussion. Keith went down to the village to phone her and try to arrange a day to pick her up and bring her over to lunch. He mentioned the missing television. "It's OK," she replied in her usual casual manner, "I've got it. I needed to check some programme tuning." She offered no apology for removing and depriving us of part of our property. She told him she'd been over to the house and had been so horrified at the state of the garden after weeks of rain, she panicked and pleaded with the gentleman who was cutting the grass in the big house to cut ours at the same time. Reluctantly he'd agreed to come over in the week and cut it. It would be rather embarrassing to have to approach him again to say the owners had cut it. She said she'd arranged for a gas engineer to come all the way over from Saintes to service the water heater for us. He would be coming on Thursday of that week. She still had no means of transport and Keith arranged to do the one-hour round trip to collect her on the Thursday and bring her over to the cottage.

The Ros who stepped out of the car that day seemed only a shadow of her former self. She explained that the process of selling her house had dragged on for nearly a year after they had signed the *compromis de vente*. Neville had refused to sign the final papers and, after postponing the inevitable until their patience ran out, the bank had been forced to repossess the house and had eventually sold it to the same English couple for one third of its market value. The couple had been a trifle embarrassed but delighted with their acquisition. Ros had found them a very pleasant couple. She told us that Neville had burned most of her clothes; she only possessed about four outfits. We asked if there was anything we could do to help but she just shrugged.

Mid afternoon a tubby little man with black hair and moustache drew up to the gate. He was the engineer who had come to service the water heater. Immediately he set to work attaching his machine to the water inlet and outlet pipes of the apparatus. When he turned on the machine the noise, which gradually rose to deafening pitch, sounded rather like stones crashing through a metal hose. We acknowledged that the water pipes to the heater must have been very badly scaled-up. As he was about to pack up his machine I reminded Ros of the reason he was there in the first place – the gas leak! Without hesitating, the man turned on the gas supply, lit a match and to our absolute horror held it up to the gas pipe, which instantly lit in three places. The engineer then turned three screws, that looked remarkably similar to the screws Mark had adjusted a year ago, and *voilà*, the leak was mended. And for that happy state of affairs and the man's trouble in coming all the way from Saintes, we were obliged to pay 780 francs. *"Mais il y a deux flames"* pointed out Ros, referring to the double pilot light. *"Oui, c'est ça"* grunted the little man. The double pilot light was normal and in practice prevented the main flame from lighting up too fiercely. Everything was fine. It was a relief.

We talked a little about Ros's situation. She had no means of transport but had four reliable friends who would happily ferry her over to the house at weekends. Two of these were available during the day should an emergency arise. It didn't seem the most satisfactory of arrangements but we had to make allowances for the unhappy situation she now found herself in. We talked about the French house insurance, and whether we were covered for any work that needed to be done to prevent the crack over the back door from worsening. Ros said she'd looked through the relevant page in the policy, and we appeared to be covered. Mark had got himself a summer job picking melons and would pay back the money he owed very soon. She said she had written to us mentioning all the things we'd talked about so there would be no need to read the letter; we could tear it up.

I had spent endless hours that week cleaning windows, paintwork, de-cobwebbing, polishing, and washing linen, cleaning floors, cutlery and crockery. There were some jobs I felt I wouldn't manage to get round to, such as cleaning food marks from the side of the cot, and cleaning the standard lamp and lampshades. Ros reassured me again that the house would be thoroughly cleaned and checked before any visitors arrived. It was an anxious time, listening to Ros's reassurances yet knowing that had we not been there that week there was no way she would have had the house ready on time, yet desperately wishing to give her the chance we felt she needed. The television was returned to us. Annoyingly Keith was obliged to spend a whole evening of our precious few days there retuning the television programmes using the French instruction book. We filled up the gas cylinder, made no mention of the broken windowpane or having to renew the bicycle saddle for the second time, and crossed our fingers.

The carpenter dropped in to have a look at the lock on the garage door, which had slipped out of alignment and wouldn't turn. Watching the carpenter, a man of reasonably small stature, effortlessly lifting off the massive doors to realign

*I had spent endless hours that week cleaning windows, paintwork,
de-cobwebbing, polishing, and washing linen, cleaning floors,
cutlery and crockery.*

them, impressed us immediately. Although we rushed forward to assist him he had the matter well in hand and we were superfluous to the task. We showed him the kitchen door whilst he was there and pointed out the crack along the wedge-shaped stone above. Unlike Monsieur Jaubert he seemed quite concerned. In pigeon French we asked if he could recommend a good *maçon* to have a look at it. He thought for a moment and nodded. He would speak to him and ask him to come over that afternoon. In the meantime he took the kitchen door off its hinges and planed the lower edge of the door to allow it to open with ease. It seemed a good moment to ask if he would be able to replace a section of the kitchen door shutters, which had rotted at the lower edge. After carefully examining each *volet* he pointed out other areas that were rotting and announced that both shutters needed replacing. He offered to make us some new shutters, and was happy to oblige us by arranging for them to be fitted in the summer during our next visit.

That afternoon, at 14.30 hours precisely, the *maçon*, a burly, tanned and balding gentleman arrived, together with a teenage boy who spoke in deliberate, hesitant schoolboy English. We showed him the cracks, inside and out, and after several tuts and frowns, he examined the stones for movement, then spoke in rapid French to his young assistant. The young boy turned to us and promised the gentleman would return in two hours with another gentleman from the *serrurerie/ferronnerie* in a village about eight kilometres away. True to his word, the man appeared later with his fellow tradesman in tow. They examined the outside of the building, the inside of the kitchen, the exterior end wall of the kitchen where an enormous crack was hidden beneath the dense Virginia creeper, and the wall of the main bedroom upstairs. After several discussions over the most appropriate solution to the problem they announced that a metal tie was necessary to fix the walls and prevent further movement. They were considering whether to place it on the inside of the building, or around the corner between two walls on the exterior. Eventually in a mixture of mime, gestures and basic French it was decided they would fix it to the outside wall. Further misunderstandings followed when I found it difficult to follow their rapid French, and understood the word *devis* to mean *de vie*. However the man gave me a gracious smile when he realised there had been a misunderstanding and eventually agreed to send me a *devis*. A visit to the insurance company in Gémozac confirmed our fears – we were not covered on the insurance for cracks appearing in the wall. The lady examined a map certifying designated disaster areas following the severe cold of the winter which, alternating with an exceptionally hot summer, had caused similar problems in the area. She then announced that if we resided in La Rochelle we would be covered but according to her official document our area was categorically not listed as a designated disaster area. Period. Our claim was turned down.

The letter Ros had posted to us just before we'd set off for France was waiting for us when we returned to the UK. It served as further confirmation that she was now not coping in her present circumstances. It stated enthusiastically that everything was fine at the cottage, the saddle had been returned and the gas cylinder replaced. She'd arranged for the water heater to be serviced. As the engineer required payment on the spot she asked us to send her a blank cheque to cover the cost. She may have meant to complete all these tasks but why was she not being completely honest with us, we wondered? Perhaps her financial situation was now so desperate she was reluctant to admit she could no longer cope. A slight unease concerning her need to deceive was developing between us, which was inhibiting our working relationship.

Towards the end of June another bombshell arrived. Ros pointed out casually that she was now back at her friend's house in the next village but one. Neville had returned from England unexpectedly and had tried to set fire to her flat. Her flat was a burned out wreck and Neville was now in a French prison charged with attempted murder and arson. According to local gossip this was a mere skeleton account of the actual event. Neville apparently had advertised his house in France, decided to accompany an interested buyer down to France in the prospective buyer's car in order to enter the country illegally, had stolen the man's car during an overnight stay, and had driven off leaving the man stranded. The metal window shutters of Ros's flat had been only partially pulled down. Neville had been able to push lighted petrol rags under the window shutters and under the door at the other end of the flat, trapping Ros in the flat. The police and fire brigade had been summoned, and when Ros was eventually rescued, she was black, dazed and severely traumatized. It was thought that as he had endangered the lives of everyone residing in the block of flats, that he would remain in prison for a long time. Although he was claiming a 'crime of passion', which in France was often legitimate grounds for acquittal, they thought in view of there being so many irate neighbours, he could possibly be given a seven-year sentence.

CHAPTER SEVEN

A DIFFICULT TASK

Ros throughout remained perfectly calm, maintaining that she had totally recovered from her ordeal, and was relieved that Neville was now in prison, and could do her and the children no further harm. We pondered on the melancholic thought that by sending Neville the money we had helped contribute in some small way to this latest horror, but as far as Ros was concerned, it was business as usual.

The June guest at the cottage who had telephoned beforehand to ask if the downstairs bed was actually a full-sized double bed as it looked a bit small in the photograph, and if the bedside lamp was strong enough to enable his wife to read in bed, then rang a second time to ask if there was a teapot at the cottage, turned out to be not quite as disagreeable as at first anticipated. The weather had been beautiful throughout (this always helps to dilute the sting of dissatisfaction) and they had spent most of their holiday in the Charente-Maritime sitting in the garden, enjoying the sunshine. Even the comment in the Visitors Book at the end of their stay that the lack of a grill at the cottage had seriously undermined their culinary activities did not worry us. There was always the barbecue!

During our summer break at the *gîte* we spent a little time cutting out a rectangular piece of turf and earth in front of the kitchen door. We then filled the area with stones and cement to allow the new kitchen door shutters to open and close freely without making contact with any long grass. Wet grass had obviously contributed to the deterioration of the lower end of the shutters, and hopefully this would lengthen the life of the new shutters. By mid-week the carpenter had not made contact and we were doubtful if at this stage he'd remembered his promise so we set off in search of his house, which was situated in a small hamlet two kilometres down the lane. His wife told us he was not at home and would we call back tomorrow lunchtime. She was a pleasant lady but we wondered if this was not one of those typical *'mañana'* fob-offs. Anxious to at least make contact we returned the next day just in time to see him drive up for the inevitable lunch break. Avoiding the various chickens that sauntered across the lane at this point, we got out of the car and he greeted us warmly. He had been very busy but no, he had not forgotten. He smiled at our worried looks. He would be over on Wednesday to fit the shutters.

Sure enough on the Wednesday morning his white van rattled up the grassy back lane and for the next hour and a half he attended to precision-fitting of the new shutters, handling them as though they were pieces of fine furniture. We were given clear instructions that they were to be given two coats of stain/preservative almost immediately. He also pointed out to us that the rusty old metal hooks dangling limply and attached to the back wall at either side of the shutters, were not broken, as we had assumed. When lifted and clicked horizontally into place they actually held the shutters back. The jutting out piece, he explained, was not a rusty knob. When cleaned up you could make out the head of a *'bergère'*. The following evening he returned with the invoice, approved the double coatings we'd already painted on the now beautifully enhanced shutters, admired the hooks, which had been cleaned up and painted black, and shyly, together with our neighbours Tom and Annabel, joined our evening festivities for a short time.

The following day the tie man arrived, confident of success in fixing the apparatus which was intended to hold the two corner walls of the kitchen together, thus preventing any further widening of the gaping and now quite alarming cracks. His little boy, at the time enjoying his *grandes vacances*, accompanied him. We had been painting the patio shutters a delicate shade of blue and had spread old English newspapers over the kitchen table to protect it from the paint pots. The little boy poured over the newspapers, deeply fascinated, reading aloud the English words with a strong French accent so the words were barely recognisable, but enjoying the attention. It wasn't a very interesting way for the child to spend his holiday, watching his father drill holes in the walls of the building. He busied himself quite happily nevertheless fetching and carrying and generally helping his father finish the work, and munching the English chocolate bars we offered from time to time to offset the boredom. The end product looked very odd. A maroon-coloured metal corner plate drilled into the wall above head height at the corner of the building was attached to a thick metal rod. This ran horizontally along the rear wall over the crack in the wall above the door, where it then turned into the house wall. At the other side of the metal plate a similar rod ran over the house wall under the thick Virginia creeper ending in a giant sized nut and bolt close to the patio door but fortunately shrouded by greenery. This needed a final adjustment. It was hard to visualise such a contraption holding the house wall together but the gentleman, who specialised in this type of work, seemed to know exactly what he was doing. After he'd gone we took out our paint brushes for the second time that day and painted the plate and the rear tie with the black metal paint. The following day we trained three long branches of the white climbing rose from the dry stone wall along the rear metal rod, as a neat disguise. The two French workmen, although expensive, had each done an excellent job and restored our faith in the punctuality and dedication of local tradesmen.

We spent the major part of the last day of our holiday cleaning, sprucing and tidying the cottage, and smartening the garden for the guests who were to follow us in. We wanted to leave Ros very little to do, to try and help her situation a little. We paid her the usual commission as though she'd done the work, although we did not ask her to check the place over, neither did she offer to. We'd noticed that the food marks were still on the side of the cot when we'd arrived, and the standard lamp and various shades had not been touched, but we

102

genuinely felt we had to make allowances at this time. Everything was left in perfect order.

The first visitors after we left were delighted with the cottage, which always made the hard work worthwhile. A fortnight after their stay I had not had the usual report form from Ros with comments and meter readings. This as a rule would have arrived on the Tuesday or Wednesday after the guests' departure, and after the return of their key to the cottage, so that as soon as the key arrived I could check the report and promptly return the deposit if all was in order. When families have been model guests delays in returning deposits are unforgivable and on this occasion I was becoming rather anxious to minimise the delay as things had moved very smoothly on our side. A little worried by her silence, I made a call to France. Ros answered, assuring me she had sent off the report form and couldn't understand why I hadn't had the letter. Her paperwork had been left in her friend's car, and if I would care to ring back the next day at 13.00 hours she'd have them ready for me. At exactly 13.00 hours the following day I phoned again. Rob answered. He'd had a party the night before and had just arisen; he had no idea where his mother was, but thought she'd gone over to her friend's house. I asked if she'd left any figures for me as she had asked me to ring at precisely that hour. There had been nothing left that he knew about. It took a third phone call before I was in possession of the required figures and was able to reassure our guests that all was well and their deposit was on its way. "You only just missed me," Ros exclaimed when I had eventually caught up with her. Why then, I wondered had she asked me to ring at precisely that hour!

The mystery was solved quite by accident days later with the return of the key from our second visiting family and their accompanying letter. Mrs. Saunders had been unable to prepare the cottage for them as the kitchen doors had been barred from the inside and she did not have a key to the garage or the French windows, as they would have expected. Fortunately the previous occupants had left the place pretty clean and they only had to defrost the fridge. They commented that they probably would have made the same mistake themselves, as our instructions did not tell them not to bar the door. I felt I should question the lady further. She told me on the phone she'd found a letter pushed under the shutters from Mrs. Saunders explaining she was locked out, therefore couldn't do the cleaning and would they mind taking their own meter readings. I took the opportunity of asking if the lawn had been cut. She replied no, there was no need; it hadn't rained and the grass hadn't grown at all. I thanked her for her time, explaining that Mrs Saunders was in possession of a full set of keys but we suspected she was having a few personal problems at the moment and was finding life rather difficult.

A few days later we returned home late in the afternoon to find a message on the answerphone from Ros. The gentleman staying in the *gîte* had phoned her to say the toilet and the shower were overflowing. She had phoned an engineer and asked him to call round but she had to go out and would not be back until 10 o'clock in the evening. We were frantic. This was an emergency. If the toilet was overflowing an emergency *fosse* clearance was necessary. It was something we couldn't sort out across the miles. It needed someone to be there. We could only wait for another message, and hope it was not bad news. At 22.15 hours we rang Ros. The plumber had not been back to her so she'd assumed everything was all right, she told us casually. The following day we had a call from France. This time it was from the gentleman staying at the cottage. He wanted to inform us that the water from the shower was not running away properly. We asked him if the toilet had been fixed. He said there was nothing wrong with the toilet; Mrs Saunders must have misunderstood his message. Had the plumber been able to sort out the problem? No plumber had called at the cottage, he confirmed. He also mentioned that a trickle of water had appeared near the kitchen step but he was mystified as to where the source of the leak was. He hoped we could manage to sort it out. We were so relieved there was no actual emergency as far as the toilet was concerned, which could have been very tricky, all other problems paled into insignificance.

It was a hopeless situation. Ros was obviously now either lying to us or being economical with the truth, pretending she was dealing with everything when in reality she was not able to cope. She had no transport, especially when it was needed. Our visitors deserved a better service than she was able to give them.

Mark had of course, no intention of paying his debt to us. If his intentions had been honourable, he would have made contact with us and worked out some means of paying us little by little, what he could afford. We would then most probably have written the debt off anyway. Instead it had become an issue, and an irritating one. The amount was trivial, but the principle was not. The ultimate responsibility, we felt, for payment of this debt lay with Ros, whose responsibility it was as key-holder and caretaker never to have flaunted that position of trust. I decided at length, the only way the issue would be resolved was to retain the final 500 francs of her commission. After all we had been paying her for all the weeks in the summer she had never set foot in the place.

I wrote to her, explaining that rather than have Mark send the money he owed us in sterling, and I send her the last amount of commission in French francs, it would be simpler all round if I held back the last payment of her commission to write off the debt. Ros, who had always neglected to see the debt as hers, reacted exactly as one who believed all along that their unique plight justified and therefore demanded unquestionable charity and absolution from sin. She was furious and threatened court action if her 500 francs were not immediately restored to her. Anyway, she insisted, we owed her 500 francs for the gardening; she'd cut the lawn twice!

In the meantime the trickle of water observed along the side of the step in the kitchen at the *gîte* was more than just a trickle.

According to our final visitor, brown liquid had now been seen running from beneath the fridge along the join in the linoleum and across the kitchen floor. They commented it was wet every day. They had mopped it up and it certainly hadn't spoiled their holiday. Mrs. Saunders had left a note explaining what had been happening and that a plumber was coming to look at it. Before they left they noticed that a brown patch was beginning to appear behind the water heater. They felt we should know about it. Ros sent the final report form with meter readings, no additional comments and no mention of the plumber.

Finally we were forced yet again to make the inevitable call to France to ask if anything had been done about the leak, as our guests had been told it was being dealt with. Ros's reaction was swift. "You won't pay me my money, but you're still asking me to do things for you." We reminded her that the problem arose during the weeks she **had** been paid for, and as far as we were concerned, no money was owed to anyone. She was determined to get the money she was owed, she exhorted, and was sending the papers off to the small claims court in England. Inevitably our conversation strayed on to potentially dangerous ground. We reminded her that we had paid her commission during the four weeks in the summer when we knew she had not been anywhere near the cottage. The atmosphere was deteriorating by the second. I indicated to Keith, who had made the fatal call, to rapidly get back on track or wind up the conversation, as we were achieving nothing. He quickly ended by saying that we were extremely worried as all the indications were that we had a burst pipe behind the wall in the kitchen, which was a very serious matter and needed emergency attention. He simply wanted to know if she'd done what she said she was going to do so we knew exactly what we were up against. She calmed a little and said she would try and get hold of Jules, the plumber, and ask him to send a *devis* for the work. We heard nothing more.

There remained at that point so little trust between Ros and myself we feared with her erratic behaviour she might try to harm us in some way and had no idea what she might do next. Certainly after her last impetuous remarks we felt our working relationship had irretrievably broken down and we should try to find another caretaker. We began faxing every acquaintance we knew of in the immediate vicinity, inquiring if they knew of anyone who would like to take on the job of caretaker to our property. One lady we faxed, who owned a property about five kilometres from the *gîte*, phoned to let us know she would be interested in the job herself. Relieved that someone had responded to our plight, we told her we would arrange to meet her at half term.

October half term arrived. We knew we had a full week ahead of us, and an unpleasant task to perform. It had rained endlessly for days, with gale force winds making the journey to the Shuttle most unpleasant. We had picked up Tilly from her Saturday morning activities and raced down the motorway in poor visibility to make the 2 o'clock Shuttle. At the slip road leading to the Shuttle the traffic came almost immediately to a halt. Bad weather reports were being circulated on the radio, announcements of reported delays and queues of up to one and a half hours to reach the ticket barrier, plus a further delay of up to one hour to board the Shuttle. We groaned. Ferries had been cancelled due to bad weather and two trains had broken down in the tunnel that day. Trains for some unknown reason were running with only two thirds of their passenger capacity. We hadn't eaten lunch and both Keith and Tilly needed the toilet. Eventually they braved the rain and walked the half-mile down to the terminal building, huddled beneath the umbrella. By the time they returned I'd edged the car forward just eight metres in the queue! The rain continued to pour and we were still not in sight of the terminal building. At 4 o'clock we eventually entered the terminal building, managed to grab something to eat, only to be called even before we'd managed to finish our meal, in order to queue again. We knew, although we had a long journey ahead of us we couldn't change our minds and return home as we had our various pressing problems to

We made the best of a bad situation and finally boarded the Shuttle at nine o'clock in the evening. We had expected to catch one at 2pm.

sort out at the *gîte*. We had books and various games with us and we knew we could only make the best of a particularly bad situation. That situation became desperate when they announced yet another train had broken down in the tunnel. We finally boarded the Shuttle at 9 o'clock in the evening. Once safely on the continent, all cars we noticed were turning towards Calais/Folkestone. Only one car turned foolishly south towards the motorway for a long journey through the night!

At Rouen the river was flooded and we drove through the heaviest rain we'd ever encountered on the continent. High winds meant that traffic was reduced to a crawling single lane crossing the viaducts, and motorway driving was hazardous and slow. We finally reached the end of our nightmare journey at 6.30 in the morning. Even at that hour our numbed brains could comprehend the severity of the damage caused by the burst pipe in the kitchen. Chairs had been upended on to the kitchen table and the table moved away from the worst of the damaged area. There was a dark brown stain behind and to the side of the water heater principally covering approximately one square metre of the plasterboard wall but the stain had splattered a little way beyond that area. A dark brown liquid trickled across the kitchen floor along the join in the linoleum. To make matters worse, the water would not turn off properly at the mains. Dawn was just beginning to break when we eventually laid our heads down on our pillows that morning.

We slept soundly in spite of our traumas until almost lunchtime, when it was time to reflect and take a closer look at the damage. The trouble had started shortly after the water heater had been serviced at the end of May. I remembered how the engineer had furiously set about dislodging the scale in the water pipes leading to the apparatus and the dreadful noise that ensued. That had to be the underlying cause of the problem. We had to attempt to turn the water off at the mains, and use it only with caution and when absolutely necessary. We were emphatically aware that each time we turned the tap on yet more water oozed out through the wall. Jules had posted a *devis* for the work into our post-box. It seemed an unfortunate coincidence that the plumber happened to be the boy friend of the lady in the next village but one, with whom Ros happened to be staying at the time. In small communities like ours, in which everyone knew each other, Jules was probably the only plumber. The estimate for the work seemed extortionately high but in the short time we had available we had very little choice in the matter. We took the piece of paper and drove into Gémozac to find out if our insurance company would accept the figures. The same garrulous blonde lady who had aborted our earlier claim over the crack in the wall greeted us with the hostile politeness of one who was about to be deprived of her personal salary. She read the *devis* carefully, ignored the fact that we were struggling with our French and poured out her rapid vocabulary at the impotent onlookers, finally throwing her hands up in despair, then picking up the phone she spoke to her colleague. Afterwards she strolled daintily over to where we were sitting looking rather sheepish, and spoke slowly for the first time.

"*Monsieur vous visitera demain, à midi.*"

I thanked her and ushered the family out of the door.

"They are going to assess the damage tomorrow," I repeated to my husband. "Let's hope they will accept Jules' *devis*."

Shortly after mid-day the following day, a distinguished-looking gentleman with grey hair and no English drew up in front of the garden gate and we swiftly ushered him through the lounge into the kitchen. He peered passively at the brown patch on the wall, examined the wet floor, the warped plinths at the base of the units, and asked how much of the wall needed to be replaced. It was easier to point to the area of wall rather than attempt to explain. He pointed out there would be a 1000 franc *franchise* to pay, wrote down the final insurance figure, shook hands and left. We quickly signed the *devis*, wrote a short note to Jules, imploring him that we would be most grateful if he could at least start the work before the end of the week, but if this was impossible, to please let us know by Tuesday of that week. We knew it would not take him out of his way to drop in a note; he passed our house every morning to pick up the messages on his answerphone and then again each evening on his way to his girl-friend's house for dinner. Predictably there was no message until we were finally obliged to ring Ros's friend, who promised she would get him to call round the next day.

On the Tuesday we'd arranged a visit from the lady who had approached us after receiving our fax inquiry concerning a caretaker. Her name was Yvonne. She lived just ten minutes away by car, rented out her own *gîte* and had lived in France for about eighteen months. She arrived looking thin and worried and we tried to put her at her ease. Within five minutes of greeting us she announced she'd have to be perfectly honest with us; she was feeling rather stressed as she was in the process of divorcing her husband. Her husband had turned up out of the blue, she'd had to leave him at the house but had no idea quite what he was up to and was most concerned at his unannounced visit. I did not dare glance at Keith at this point; I was sure we were both thinking "Oh no, not again." By this time we were all feeling rather agitated. Having got her there I did not want her to rush off in case she failed to return and we'd lost possibly our only chance of finding a replacement caretaker, and she was obviously not at all relaxed, counting the minutes she was away from the house. We had noticed the *gîte* she advertised was newly renovated and asked if they had done all the work themselves. They had bought the house eighteen months previously, she continued, from a couple who had completed the renovations when their marriage had broken up and they'd felt obliged to sell up.

We wondered why it was that this pattern seemed to be continually repeated among couples who came to live in France. We believed people often emigrated in the hope of escaping threats of redundancy, financial problems or even the sheer boredom of their personal lives. Having made the decision often one of the partners either didn't like the quiet country life, could not make an adequate living, or could not easily master the language difficulties. Thus there emerged an instant recipe for disaster. Yvonne loved the country, spoke the language well and was happy living in France; her husband found it difficult to settle, and spent more and more time away from home.

She looked around the house and we showed her the various quirks involved, most of which she felt she could deal with. Her biggest worry was that her husband would find out about it, which would affect the amount of alimony she would receive. Our worry was that we would be surrendering to a fate that took us straight out of the frying pan into the fire. But at least she had been honest with us from the beginning, and that was refreshingly new. We acknowledged we must not prejudge her and must give her a fair chance. She apologised and announced that she really could not stay any longer but would return at the same time on Thursday to finish seeing the house and assured us she was perfectly trustworthy and would do a good job for us. She asked if we could send her the contract to study after November 9th, by which time her husband would have left. As French houses are notoriously difficult to find, we made arrangements for my husband to follow her in his car so we would know how to find her house when we needed to. This had to be done discreetly so as not to alert suspicion on the part of her husband. We were far from happy with the situation but felt we were left with little alternative.

The following day we decided to meet head on the task we had been dreading. Somehow we had to try to persuade Ros to give up the keys to the cottage, something we felt she would be reluctant to do. We had reason to believe that if we sacked her and then demanded the return of the keys she would dig her heels in and either make the excuse that they were not in her possession at that particular moment, or say she had lost them. With the keys in her possession she had access to free accommodation whenever she chose, a thought that terrified us – she might even claim squatters' rights, if such a thing existed in France. Months of suffering vicious assaults combined with sheer desperation had so changed her personality and alienated her from honesty and decency we could no longer recognise the kindly lady who had taught Tilly how to play card games and welcomed us to her home. We therefore found ourselves undertaking such underhand trickery to secure the safe return of the keys. The alternative was to change all the locks in the house, a task too long and cumbersome to undertake in the little time we had there, and one that would also entail having new duplicate keys made for visitors and other keyholders. Soon after buying the house I recall Keith had attached an expensive lock on to the patio door. He had been faced with the complicated task of having to reverse the lock before attaching it to the shutters; the parts had been so intricate the whole operation had taken three days. We certainly did not relish having to repeat this procedure.

We set out with glum faces for the half-hour drive to Ros's flat. We would try to catch her unawares; this had worked in the past. She appeared entirely unmoved by our presence, almost as though she was expecting us. In appearance she seemed rather thin and hunched, even shorter in stature than I remembered her, with heavy make-up disguising her gaunt features. She showed us in to the small but not unpleasant sitting room of her flat. This pitiful shadow of a figure, lacking the dignity she once possessed, was not at all her former self. I wanted to hug her, but at the same time she terrified me, and I desperately wished we could turn back the clock and start again. We exchanged formalities, then proceeded to spend the next one and a half hours in a nightmare of small talk, playing with the kitten, making a fuss of the dog, trying to appear natural and informal, yet being oddly aware that she knew exactly why we were there. She apologised for the state of her flat; the insurance company was apparently still haggling over the redecoration required in her hallway resulting from fire damage. She said Rob was receiving letters from his father who was still in prison. He was pressurising Rob to go and see him but Rob had no desire to visit him, and was becoming quite upset by his continued persistence. She explained that she would normally pull down the metal blinds but on that particular day it was stifling hot and she had left the blinds open about two inches. Neville had managed to slide lighted petrol rags under the blind and set fire to the flat. Now that he was locked away in prison she could open the windows again and sleep easily in her bed at night. She asked if Jules had left a *devis* and we explained we were trying to pin him down to do the work. This was our cue to ask if we could possibly have her set of keys to give to him, as it was looking likely that he would not be able to complete the work that week. Without hesitation she suggested that she could give him the keys herself, as she would be seeing her friend that week. Not to worry, I said, we would be seeing him and could give him the set of keys ourselves if she'd like to give them to us.

She stared at me, disbelievingly. She lowered her voice. "You don't trust me, do you," she suddenly flashed.

"Look, Ros," I said calmly, "I'd like to have the set of keys. They're our property and I've decided to call in the keys."

"I don't have them," she snapped, her voice quite changed, "they're in my friend's car."

She said her friend could probably drop them off to us later in the week, but that, we felt was not at all satisfactory and most probably wouldn't happen. Instead we suggested we wouldn't want to put her friend to such trouble and would call again. In that case if we could ring her after 19.00 hours that evening she promised she would give us a time when we could collect them. We were entirely sceptical about the arrangement but had no choice but to go along with it. She knew my husband to be a completely honest man and hopefully would not dare waste too much of his time playing silly games. On that note we departed.

I was panicking.

"She's not going to hand the keys over," I thought aloud.

"We're only here for five days and we're having to spend two of them coaxing Ros to hand over our keys."

The following day, after speaking to Ros from the phone box in the village, we made the one hour round trip to her flat again this time at the requested hour. I was so sure that she would not hand over a full set of keys, I'd rummaged through the car's glove compartment and managed to find the dictaphone that we kept there. My thoughts were racing. If she failed to hand over the keys I would record her excuse so we'd have some ammunition to prove that she was attempting deliberately to withhold our keys. We sat in the car trying to pluck up courage to ring the doorbell. We asked Tilly to stay in the car, explaining that we wouldn't be long. Ros answered almost immediately, and much to our surprise, immediately produced the bunch of keys. "The only thing is," she exclaimed casually, " the garage door key seems to be missing!"

A vortex of thoughts swirled in our minds as we left – relief that at least part of our mission had been accomplished and we could now move forward, pity in view of her dire circumstances, anger because we were all aware the key was in Mark's possession, and guilt that we couldn't do more to help her. One fact we felt very sure about; it was inevitably the end of our working relationship. We called in at the *bricolage* on the way back to pick up three strong bolts for the garage door. Hopefully those and the weight of the garden seat against the garage door would thwart any potential intruders over the winter months at least. We had taken with us to France a letter officially terminating her contract as caretaker, and this we eventually posted to her.

At this time of year in France the *boutiques de fleuriste*, the *supermarchés* and *les pépinières* were ablaze with colour, displaying the most wonderful pots of magnificent chrysanthemums, ranging from tiny single flower-heads to huge spectacular doubles in magenta, bronze, crimson and bright yellow. It was a spectacular sight and we were very tempted on one occasion to purchase a pot of these beautiful flowers to take to a neighbour we were visiting that evening. We were however, being totally ignorant of the fact that the flowers were produced to celebrate All Souls Day when relatives travel huge distances to lay flowers on the graves of their relatives and dear ones. Much as we were tempted to buy a pot it would not have been appropriate to flaunt tradition in that way, and we were content to merely admire the spectacular arrays.

Yvonne did not turn up to finish her tour of the house. Jules did not make an appearance either, and we were becoming exceedingly frustrated. At about nine o'clock that evening, after we had closed up the shutters for the night, there was a loud banging at the kitchen door shutters. We opened the door and could just about recognise Jules' face in the complete darkness. Having an English girl-friend he delighted in the chance to show off his English, which was adequate if not accomplished. If we attempted to speak to him in French he inevitably answered in English. The result was strangely comical and we eventually submitted and spoke only in English. We were relieved to see him even at that late hour. He managed to confirm that he'd made a hole in the plasterboard to see quite what he was up against and there was indeed a burst pipe. He would have to remove the water heater from the wall, take down a large section of the plasterboard, repair the pipe, replace the damaged plasterboard and reconnect the water heater. There was no way he could fit in the work that week but if we could leave him the key he would be able to do it in about a fortnight's time and could either post the key back to us or give it to Ros.

This posed a further dilemma. Jules had no idea that Ros was no longer our caretaker. She could turn up at the house while he was doing the work, calmly take the bolts off the garage door and even walk off with the spare set of keys. I ruled nothing out after the experience we'd had with Mark. My imagination was working overtime. We tried to explain to Jules that Ros was no longer our caretaker, and any keys we deposited with him were for his use only and must not be passed on to anyone, neither must he let anyone into the house. Quite how much he understood we didn't know, but he looked rather perplexed.

Thursday came and went and there was still no sign of Yvonne, not even a message of apology and we were anxious enough to drive to the village and telephone her. A male voice answered and he passed the phone on to Yvonne. The moment she recognised our voices she seemed taken aback.

"Oh, yes – er, I'll take it in the other room..."

There was a pause and suddenly the line went dead. Further attempts to try to reach her were answered by repeated engaged tones. Finally we had to give up. The scenario bore such worrying similarities to our last experience we were unsure whether to get out quick or explore further. Finally we were coerced into trying once more to make sense of the situation for our own satisfaction. The night before our departure we rang again. This time Yvonne answered the phone, sounding extremely vague and rather distant. She explained that she'd had an infection that had 'knocked her for six', was on her third course of antibiotics and felt extremely miserable and lethargic. She told us not to worry, if she found she could not look after the *gîte* for us she would definitely find someone who could. We wrote to her after November 9th as promised, with all the details enclosed. Seven weeks later we received a large envelope. Inside was my letter, the contract, the details, plus the briefest of notes from Yvonne indicating that she would not now be able to look after the cottage after all, and that she felt sure we would find someone else soon. Quite what was behind her sudden change of heart we were never to find out. Although it plunged us into further crisis we found ourselves strangely relieved.

Three weeks following our eventful half term at the cottage there was still no word from Jules and we had visions of a widening crisis in view of the faulty mains tap if the work was not done soon. In December I put in a call to France to try to find out what on earth was causing the delay. Surprisingly

Jules answered the phone. He had fallen off a ladder and hurt his back and had been off work for five weeks. At the same time he was happy to point out that his back was now fine and he would be able to do the work the following week. As Tom and Annabel were going down the following weekend for their pre-Christmas break, I asked if, when he'd finished the work he could hand the keys over to them instead of posting them on to us. They would then verify that the work had been done to a satisfactory standard and I would be able to pay the bill immediately. It was a way of encouraging him to complete the work before Christmas. We have since learned that the 'have fallen off a ladder and hurt my back' routine is used quite often in France when tradesmen fail to complete work on time. It serves to get the customer off their back while simultaneously invoking sympathy and understanding. He did however, complete the work on time and returned the key to Annabel much to our relief. A much smaller area of the plasterboard outer wall had been replaced than we had discussed, leaving a rather unsightly additional join in the plasterboard, and the tiles near the sink where the brown stain had caused the grout to discolour, had been left untouched.

Shortly after Christmas a small ray of hope appeared on the horizon. We received a telephone call from a lady who told us she had been contacted by a friend and understood we were looking for a new caretaker to look after our cottage in France, and that she might be interested in the job. She said if I would care to phone a lady, whose address and telephone number she gave me, the lady would provide her with a reference. Things were really looking up; I hadn't been offered references before. There was something about her geordie accent that sounded very genuine. She spelt out what she felt she was able to do, and what she felt she could not take on, such as gardening. She too, let out a *gîte* in the summer months, with a Saturday changeover, which left her pretty tied up on Saturdays. I sent her a copy of the contract to have a look at, emphasising that this was merely to provide a list of duties so neither side would be in any doubt as to what her responsibilities entailed, and there would be no duplication of duties. She took the contract very seriously, made several suggestions and requested one or two sensible changes, even told us she thought it was imperative to pay the guests a visit shortly after arrival. All part of the job, she believed. I believed we were going to get along. I told her I would phone her shortly before our visit in May to arrange a visit. It was becoming a ritual.

At the beginning of April the telephone suddenly rang late one evening, which sent us scurrying to our computer. It was my sister, who lived in the north-east of England, sounding rather shocked. She had been watching the television regional news bulletin and thought we should know some disturbing news. We scanned the regional news bulletin on the Internet until we found the relevant section. "Oh no! Dear God – no!" I murmured.

CHAPTER EIGHT

TRAGEDY

The news bulletin sent us reeling with shock and disbelief. It stated briefly that the mutilated body of local builder, Neville Saunders, who had recently been released from prison in France, where he had been serving a sentence for arson and attempted murder, had been found in a quarry, thirty miles from Saintes. His two sons, Mark and Robert, had been arrested and held in connection with his murder. His former wife Rosalind, together with a French friend, had been charged with attempting to dispose of the body and released on bail. The dead man and his former wife had been resident in France for seven years, it read. The news was difficult to assimilate and we read over the relevant passage several times, speculating on the details of what might have happened.

According to the story related to us later, Neville had been released from prison at the end of March, had returned to Ros's flat and insisted on seeing her, thereby violating a restraining order preventing him from approaching her, and had attempted to attack his former wife. The two boys, determined to prevent at all costs a repeat of the last occasion in which Mark and his mother had been terribly injured, were said to have had intervened, killing him. It was as though a huge black cloud had fallen on this unhappy, unfortunate and beguiled family. How would they ever find the peace of mind they had been so fervently searching and hoping for? Whatever the outcome, they would carry this burden with them for the rest of their lives.

Our thoughts were still charged with and haunted by these evocative memories when we arrived for our usual May break at the cottage. I couldn't look at the beautiful blue, beige and cream tiled bedroom floor without picturing Neville carefully laying the tiles. It was a very emotive time. I preferred to remember the two of them as they were at the time we first knew them. We had already said our good-byes, however. Now it was time to turn our thoughts momentarily elsewhere.

A sound of running water reached our ears the moment we opened the kitchen door, which much to our surprise, opened with ease. We discovered the shower had been turned on, and water was gushing into the shower base. At first the switch on the showerhead would not turn off, but eventually Keith repeated the movement, and this time it clicked and he managed to turn it off. The mains tap however, though turned fully clockwise, was still registering a flow on the water meter and would not completely isolate the water. We had no idea how long the water had been running but were shocked to discover that two hundred units of water had run away since our last visit, an immense amount of water considering a normal sized family used on average four to six units per fortnight. We therefore concluded that Jules must have used the shower to clean some of his tools when he had fixed the leak just before Christmas, had inadvertently left it running (a fact when it was suggested to him he later vehemently denied) and the water had been running continually ever since.

The problem of the gas water heater was becoming an ongoing saga, as it was still continuing to give trouble. This time, there didn't seem to be enough water pressure for the pilot light to ignite the main flame. With the thermostat turned up to its highest setting, the flame would just about light. When adjusted down to a lower setting, the gas would not light at all. Somehow, removing the apparatus from the wall and reconnecting it after fixing the burst pipe had affected it in some way. We rang Jules, left messages on his answerphone, and written notes at his house, but not until Thursday did we have any response. We seemed to be in a 'chicken and egg' situation.

Eventually he turned up at six o'clock on the Thursday evening on his way home. He thought as the water had been left running continually (but not by him!) the apparatus had become badly scaled up again and needed a further service, for which he then offered his assistance. He carried in a large pump with attached plastic tubes, connected the free ends of the tubes to the water heater and switched on. The usual noisy clattering sound on this occasion was entirely absent and he shook his head with dismissive faith in the state of our water-heater, announcing the apparatus had completely scaled up, until it occurred to him that it was his rather pathetic descaling apparatus that was blocked up. He quickly informed us that the machine did not belong to him; he had just borrowed it as his own machine was not working properly. Finally he announced he'd have to go and collect his own machine as it would work better than the one he was using. Leaving the faulty apparatus attached to the even more faulty cure, he sped off down the lane towards the village.

Twenty minutes later he returned with his own hastily revamped machine to complete the service. After having the stuffing knocked out of the water heater for the second time in a year the apparatus seemed marginally improved, but this time the pilot light wouldn't light automatically and could only be lit using a long taper. His excuse was that sometimes the pilot light can suddenly fail and would be very expensive to replace. The gas ignited on the correct setting but the flame was nowhere near as powerful as it should have been and the water was barely hot. I was not at all happy but he seemed to think it was working fine and we told him we'd see how things went. He charged us yet another 450 francs, which on later studying the *facture*, I then discovered included the travel time he'd spent collecting his less than perfect machine from his house. The water heater continued to give trouble. Jules avoid-ed insouciantly all attempts to persuade him to return and take a further look at the apparatus, even inferring the machine was old and needed replacing anyway!

During our visit we arranged to see Liz, the lady who had contacted us about looking after our house, and Colin, her husband. We'd chatted a few times on the phone and by the time we met I already felt I knew them. Being a small farming community she had already gathered who our previous caretaker had been. Her daughter, who went to the same school as Rob, had been very upset by the incident. We explained that Ros had ceased to look after the cottage even before the incident occurred but nevertheless we'd been quite affected by it. The family had lived in France for four years. Her daughter was more at home speaking French than English. They too, had a *gîte* that they occasionally let out to holidaymakers in the summer, and seemed well attuned to the requirements of the job. Her husband spoke fluent French. They both did a tour of the house, and I pointed out where all the spares were kept and wrote down the telephone numbers of various tradesmen who had in the past dealt with things that could go wrong occasionally. They loved the house and agreed at least for the time being to act as our caretakers, providing we could find someone to do the garden.

That opportunity arose mid-week when we were attempting to replace the old garden gate, which was becoming far too dangerous. The metal catch had sheared off the old gate and was impossible to replace. One had to be a genius in order to close the gate without both halves overlapping in the middle. One of the concrete gate-posts had broken close to its base, the old white iron gate was rusty in parts, covered in a green lichen which had become ingrained in the white paint and on the whole it had seen better days. We had studied books with gates of standard sizes and it soon became evident that we'd have to order gates specially constructed for us. The space was too wide to take a standard single size and too small for a standard pair. To save time therefore, we had purchased a pair of black double wrought iron gates with matching posts in England and had brought them down with us. The broken concrete post proved to be more difficult to remove than we had anticipated. Both posts were firmly embedded in deep concrete. We had hammers, mallets and chisels but nothing quite strong enough to chip away the concrete. Eventually the Englishman who managed *la grande maison blanche* in the owners' absence, on hearing our curses, wandered over to see if he could help. Amongst his tools he happened to have just the tool we needed and he very kindly stayed to give us a hand breaking up the concrete, a task we could never have completed alone. He introduced himself as Kevin, said he was often around the hamlet and if we needed anything else doing he'd be pleased to help. Before we left at the end of the week he had trimmed the Virginia creeper away from the roof, as for the second time in three years the creeper was growing underneath and in danger of loosening the Roman roof tiles, or *tuiles canals*, as they are often known. He also offered to cut the grass and keep the garden tidy for us during our absence.

Keith did an excellent job setting the gateposts and hanging the gates, making numerous meticulous checks with the spirit level after each successive trowel full of concrete was carefully placed in the hole. We were proud of our smart new gates that matched the wrought-iron ties at the front and rear of the cottage, and by an encouraging hand of fate, we'd found ourselves a gardener. Our final task, before making our way back to the Shuttle, was to drop the keys off to Liz and inform her of the good news.

Our summer break at Le Petit Hameau, we decided, was to be spent enjoying the countryside and doing pleasurable things. Tilly had her old bike back, which was immediately relegated to the person least in need (me), in favour of the new mountain bike she had been given for her birthday and which on this occasion we had brought with us. Keith was even less fortunate, being designated a rusty old bike, lent to us by Liz, which had been left out in the rain and was conspicuously much too small for him. Oblivious to the bemused looks from the local people, the comically tantalising trio set off along the narrow country lanes to explore the villages and hamlets in the area. A house in one of the villages we passed had a large round stone table in the garden which was almost always occupied by a huge sleeping Alsatian who peered up warily without moving

The mere presence of us on our bikes roused a chorus of dogs barking and chickens squawking. An engaging smile, and three consecutive 'bonjours', was enough to win over the lady taking in her washing.

his head as we cycled by. Our mere presence passing through their villages we soon discovered, was enough to arouse a chorus of dogs barking, geese laying, chickens squawking and a hive of farmyard activity at this unparalleled disruption to their peace. An engaging smile and three consecutive *bonjours* in passing, was enough to win over the lady watering her flower-trough or taking in the contents of her washing-line. Apart from the sore rears and aching limbs expected of those whose fitness might well be in question, we had a splendid day.

During our stay we visited the Abbey ruins, Chapter Room, Scriptorium and Chapels of the Monastery at Fondouce situated in a tranquil setting at Brie-des-Bois just north-east of Saintes. The modest entry fee included a glass of *pineau des Charentes* at the end of the tour, although Tilly missed out on the honours, much to her disgust. The Abbaye at Sablonceaux was also a lovely venue for an afternoon visit, with its famous black walnut tree, one of the most beautiful in France, under which two hundred people were known to have been seated for supper. We revisited Talmont, a popular and pretty village of small white shops with shutters painted in beautiful pastel shades, displaying local crafts including pottery, paintings, soaps, jewelry and crystal. We strolled through the narrow pedestrian-only lanes among the tall brightly coloured hollyhocks towards the small Romanesque church situated on a promontory overlooking the Gironde estuary. The church, impressive against a background of shimmering sea, is incomplete as the nave subsided into the sea several years ago. The remaining section has been underpinned.

Another port of call, Pons, a medieval town, has a large fortress with ramparts and a passage beneath the ramparts. Standing on one of the bridges in the centre of the town one could follow the river and make out the old *tannerie* on one side of the bridge and a privately owned working water mill on the other side. A truly impressive *vieille ville*. Occasionally while travelling through France one can make out one of those peculiar *Lanterne des Morts* found only in France, and one particularly good example can be found at Fenioux. The Romanesque structure symbolises eternal light and glorification of the dead, and is made up of eleven large upright stone columns above which is a small lantern and spire, with thirty-seven spiral stone steps leading up to the lantern. The church at Fenioux dates back to Carolingian times, one wall of which is ninth century.

Our holiday of course, would not have been complete without the occasional trips to the beaches at Meschers, beautiful sandy, pine-backed bays, very popular with the French, and further north can be found the tourist beaches of Royan and la Grande-Côte. Much as we enjoyed a day at the beach, it was always a great joy to return to the tranquillity of the cottage and an evening barbecue. We bought a couple of loungers that summer in order to make the most of our time spent enjoying the garden.

One day we dropped off at the antique shop in Boutenac-Touvent. The shop, which seemed to be permanently open, was run by a tall swarthy gentleman, who when he wasn't hard at work renovating furniture, was always to be seen seated in front of his shop surveying the constant stream of traffic travelling along the main Bordeaux route. On this occasion he was hard at work in his workshop as we browsed around the shop. The chairs seemed much too grand for the purpose we had in mind and we indicated that we were looking for old chairs for painting. He gestured to an older lady in the back of the shop and indicated to us to follow him to his *atelier*. We followed him to an old workshop a short distance down the road, where he unlocked the door of the building, revealing an old house bursting with dusty old furniture, piled up in enormous heaps: broken cupboards, tables with loose legs, chairs with broken seats and furniture riddled with woodworm. He lifted away enough furniture to clear a space just wide enough to reach the light switch, then indicated that we could see if there was anything we liked. We spent about half an hour in the house, clambering over furniture, picking up samples of chairs and discarding others that had been well and truly punished by woodworm infestation. Eventually we settled for two matching chairs that appeared to be free of woodworm and a third of dainty design, with studded areas on the seat and backrest. We carried the goods to the shop entrance; the man nodded, charged us a mere 50 francs for each of the three chairs, and we piled them into the car, well pleased with our bargains.

The following day we took the chairs out into the garden, cleaned them up a little, and painted them a beautiful jade green, then painted the legs of the kitchen table the same colour. The effect was simple but quite stunning. All we needed now was a fourth chair to complete the set. We'd been told of a large antique warehouse just outside Pons, often open at odd times during the day even during the idle hour when normally the whole of France comes to an extended halt – lunchtime – and we decided to pay them a visit. The warehouse contained everything from old bicycles, rusty old tools, to perfect period pieces of furniture. As we sauntered around I managed to come across a matching chair to the two we'd already bought, although it wasn't in nearly such pristine condition, and I was ecstatic. I carried the chair up to the desk and asked how much he would charge for the mottled-looking affair. He smiled one of those wry smiles and replied *"deux cents cinquante francs."* My mouth dropped. I tried to explain that I'd bought two similar chairs at another shop and had only been charged 50 francs for each but the man was not interested. I pointed out the chair was in poor condition and was not worth 250 francs and picked up a genuine antique chair that was priced at 300 francs to make a realistic comparison but the man only shrugged. For some reason he did not wish to sell us the chair at a reasonable price, and we left empty-handed and disappointed. The next day we returned to the antique shop in Boutenac-Touvent, fought our way further into the old workshop and chose a fourth chair, not the one we would have preferred, but nevertheless a bargain at 50 francs.

A chance encounter with Kevin mid-week revealed there had been a problem at the barn. He had gone to check the house over when he'd noticed water oozing under the door. The ground floor of the barn consisted mainly of one enormous room, one end of which was the kitchen. Tom and Annabel had very cleverly installed a peninsular unit across the room at the kitchen end to form a proper kitchen area. Across the room overhanging the peninsular unit Tom had fixed a string of halogen lamps, the effect of which looked very cosy and pretty. At the kitchen end of the room were two mains water taps, one of which did not turn off properly. They had invited friends to stay, leaving a list of instructions and closing down procedures. Somehow the visitors had closed off the wrong mains tap, there had been a leak, water had poured out directly on to the lovely pink-beige room tiles, and the whole room was flooded with water to a depth of six inches. Kevin, assisted by Audrey, had donned Wellington boots, turned the water off at the correct mains and cleaned up the floor as best they could.

We'd noticed Tom and Annabel arrive the day after us and were surprised that almost a week had gone by and, apart from a friendly wave along the back lane as we simultaneously opened up our shutters one morning, we had not seen them even to pass the time of day, which was most unusual. Eventually Annabel wandered over to the cottage, looking dazed and rather dishevelled. We persuaded her to join us on the patio and poured her out a glass of wine. She sank exhausted into the seat and told us they had not stopped from the moment they'd arrived. She had planned to have a relaxing holiday but instead had found herself washing curtains and covers and cleaning up items damaged in the flood. In spite of several washes the curtains and covers still had permanent water marks six inches from their lower edges and they could not seem to lose the unwholesome dank smell that persisted everywhere. Although she was still smiling she certainly had not planned to spend her summer holiday in this manner.

The barn with its huge open-plan living room occupying most of the ground floor was much more characteristically French than could be said of our property. Both houses had stone walls almost two feet thick, which kept the insides very cool during the overwhelmingly hot summer months. Conversely they were well insulated in the winter. The barn was very dark inside, as are most Charentaise houses, the only light being afforded by an entry door at the side near the kitchen end of the room, and a small French window at the opposite short end of the room. Two quaint little windows, with equally tiny shutters each no more than twelve inches square, were the only other sources of natural light in the room. Annabel, with her artistic flair and an instinctive eye for decor, knew exactly what needed to be done. The wooden open staircase, which led up to the upper floor from the inner side of the open-plan room gave the lucky person who happened to be ascending the stairs, an unaccustomed view of the occupants in the bedroom below. The French window, on the other hand, was rather superfluous, and opened up onto an exotic view of the high hedge (and beyond that a three year old redundant rotting haystack), which provided them with the necessary privacy from the lane. Annabel's brilliant idea was to change the use of the ground floor bedroom and turn it into a lounge, knock out part of the outer wall of the 'lounge' and locate a new arched French window overlooking the garden with its splendid view of the rolling countryside beyond. It was an ingenious idea and worked well. The area outside the new French window was turned into a patio and this then led directly to the swimming pool area.

One day while Annabel's sister and family were holidaying at the barn, her sister took a long look at the chairs which the artistic Annabel had painstakingly painted bright turquoise with an unusual feathered finish and decided to repaint them a startling bright yellow. Instead of being devastated at having her handywork dismissed in this manner, Annabel loved the new look and reflected that she could quite see the point her sister was trying to make. The rapport between the two sisters was astonishing and quite unique.

We had at various times confronted, been fascinated by, and enjoyed an enormous variety of wildlife during our visits to the cottage, and Annabel no longer used black bin-liners to protect the plants after they had come to the conclusion that the plastic seemed to attract the numerous black grass snakes often seen in the region. The sight of one of these snakes would induce Annabel's sister to study the creature from a safe distance, book in hand, to discover if the specimen was potentially poisonous. Whenever we stayed at the *gîte* we always made a point of opening up all the doors and windows in order to keep the place aired, as so often the house was closed up for months at a time. On one occasion I was rummaging in the ground floor bedroom when I was startled by the sudden presence there of an enormous salamander, bright green in colour, about eighteen inches long, with hefty limbs and staring eyes. For a moment I froze in horror, until I recognised that the poor innocuous creature was as fearful of me as I was of this unwelcome intruder. I dashed to the garage to grab my husband, but on returning there was absolutely no sign of the giant beast. Keith searched vigilantly, turning the bedroom upside down but the creature had vanished. I was certain that it was still in the bedroom hiding somewhere and would not go to bed that night until once again every inch of bed clothing had been thoroughly examined. The following afternoon, with the incident forgotten, I ventured once again into the bedroom and stared in amazement as the salamander slowly crept into view from behind Keith's size eleven shoe. Again the creature disappeared as quickly as it had appeared, and has never been seen since. I think the family would prefer to think the creature was a figment of my imagination but my privileged viewing of this amazing creature to this day remains a uniquely personal experience.

I was working in the kitchen one day during the summer

holidays when suddenly we heard the shriek of Tilly's voice sounding somewhat distressed. We hurried upstairs to find Tilly rooted to the spot, gazing disbelievingly at a thick line of marching black ants which led across the room in a straight line between the open floor-resting window and the bedside table. They continued up the leg of the table and across to the glass of lemon juice she'd left on her bedside table. The incident cured her of the habit of taking sweet drinks up to bed.

Generally speaking the wildlife presence in the area was one of the attractions of staying at the cottage. One day we were fascinated by the presence of a pale green praying mantis, with its heart-shaped slightly flattened head and comparatively large eyes staring up to heaven. We wondered if the poor creature was offering a short prayer on our behalf over the continuing malfunction of the wretched water-heater! Occasionally we would see a plumed game bird seated on the stone seat outside on the patio. Fortunately our resident pests, the moles, had left us and found an alternative home over at the barn, which pleased them not a great deal. Aerating the garden was fine, but in their regular habit of tossing over the plants they were a definite nuisance. Another, more gentle creature habitually present in the garden was the tiny tree frog, no more than two centimetres in length before stretching out its legs, and a distinctive pastel green in colour with a contrasting peach-coloured patch. The frogs would provide us with a twilight serenade of noisy high pitched honks. It was hard to imagine such tiny creatures providing such grand fortissimos, one enterprising visitor referring to them as 'the barbecue trio'. Small bats were also frequent visitors in the twilight hours, and could be seen flying harmlessly overhead between the trees during our candlelit dinners on the patio. In summer the elusive red admirals and large exquisite black and white striped butterflies could be seen hovering over the fragrant lavender bush.

We received the unexpected news one day that Audrey and her husband had made a decision to sell *la grande maison blanche*. We were entirely surprised knowing the amount of time, effort and planning that had gone into the renovation work and Audrey's obvious pleasure in watching her ideas grow to fruition. Apparently her husband preferred to own a house somewhere a little more conveniently situated in order to visit for frequent short breaks instead of feeling obliged to spend the whole summer there. The sad fact was that there was no way they would even get a return on their investment. The house was worth less than the purchase price plus the money they had paid out on the installations and renovations, something British buyers often found it hard to come to terms with. Audrey had always enjoyed her holidays at Le Petit Hameau and used always to be seen taking her lone stroll across the fields before breakfast. Her husband used to joke that back home Audrey would never normally touch French bread; here in France, he couldn't keep her off it!

Here I had to admit that not only did I enjoy a fresh *baguette* for breakfast, but I simply adored the *brioche Vendéene* such as is found only in France, a slightly sweet soft bread made with eggs that simply melts in the mouth. Sometimes lunch would consist of a *baguette* with the conical *fromage de chèvre, Roquefort,* or *St Paulin,* our favourite French cheeses, with huge slices of tasty locally-grown tomatoes, followed by the most delicious melon in the world – the pale and dark green striped *melon Charentais,* with its apricot coloured flesh. All this washed down with a Bordeaux wine or, in the case of Tilly, a fresh peach juice or Orangina. An unusual cheese cake, the *torteau de fromager* with its convex black crust due to it being baked in a very hot oven, could also be found in this part of France.

One evening we heard there was a firework display taking place in the village that night, and everyone would be gathering in the *place* at ten o'clock. We drove down towards the normally quiet village and, leaving the car on the outskirts, we sauntered towards the church where large crowds were gathering. Some of the familiar *artisans*, there with their families, nodded in recognition. Shortly after ten o'clock a few of the local people, carrying pretty lanterns on rods formed a double line to escort a rather ragged-looking band along the lane out of the village. The crowd followed immediately the band struck up and everyone formed a happy column behind the leaders. Finally the parade turned into a field, and the crowd spread out over a corner of the field to listen to the band play. This was followed by an exciting display of fireworks, after which the band struck up once again before the crowd finally dispersed. We had been made to feel part of the community at last, and it was a feeling that was rather special.

An encouraging sign was that our visitors that summer, however hard they tried, could find very little to complain about and there were wonderful comments in the Visitors' Book, reporting how they had found the cottage and its environment delightful, and had found so much of interest in the area. That, in spite of the water heater being not quite as it should be, was enormously exhilarating. People had of course, had to turn the thermostat up to the highest setting to produce hot water which was worrying, and we'd come to the conclusion that we'd have to try to get hold of the manufacturer's official engineer to take a look at it. There has never been a season when some small annoying little incident didn't take place and this one was no exception. Liz had mentioned that the final guests were not happy about the toilet seat, without actually mentioning what was wrong with it. We arrived for our autumn visit to find the toilet seat had been broken yet again and the culprits had attempted their own intriguing remedy by churlishly sticking it up with Sellotape. Liz had not mentioned the matter as she thought we had left it like that, therefore finding approaching the subject rather embarrassing but we were eventually able to persuade her that we would not deliberately debase her role in this fashion. This time we had the choice of the type of seat needed, paid a visit to the local *bricolage*, bought a solid compressed-wood toilet seat and fixed it, we hoped, for the final time.

I had decided it would be the last summer we spent there in

the company of that disgusting *fosse* cover. Two of the corners were now crumbling badly, occasionally leaking obnoxious fumes into the garage even with a disguising wrap of underlay and linoleum. I had carefully measured the lid and in September set about manufacturing a new lid, constructing a frame made out of orange boxes given to me by the kind man on the fruit stall at the market. The measurements had to be precise to the last millimetre for the lid to be a perfect fit – an absolute essential. I placed the frame on a cardboard base, covered it in black polythene and filled the frame with three centimetres of fine concrete and wire mesh, the latter to strengthen the finish. Into the concrete I embedded a central black iron plate and hook, smoothed off the top surface, and waited for the concrete to dry. The result was unbelievably realistic. The final touch was to paint the top in a similar sand-coloured concrete paint to that covering the floor of the garage. Painting the garage floor was a whim we had indulged in earlier, in an attempt to brighten up the garage and keep the dust down. Unfortunately the store no longer produced the beautiful soft blue concrete paint we'd had our eye on. We were forced to choose, as the blandest of the colours remaining, what appeared on the label as 'sand' but turned out to be a rather unsavoury bilious yellow which did not do justice to or in any way enhance, the garage floor! With a little chipping required at one edge, the lid was eventually made to fit perfectly. I was allowed to indulge in a little pride over my small work of art, and for the first time we had a hook with which to lift the cover, and which would make life a little easier for the man whose job it was to complete the *vidange*.

The three cracked window panes, two of which were not too badly cracked and were exhibiting slight cracks when we bought the house, were still patiently awaiting replacement, and this time we'd come prepared. Having carefully measured the window panes in the lounge we'd brought the ready-cut tiny panes with us and Keith set about one sunny autumn afternoon the delicate task of knocking out the broken glass in preparation for inserting the new glass. It was a painstakingly slow task for an amateur, especially the puttying, it being exceptionally difficult to obtain a straight, smooth surface with not too many fingermarks on the glass. With one pane in and not looking too amateurish it was time for a celebratory glass of beer, or cooling off time as truth to tell, it was hot, thirsty work. When it came to the next two panes we were surprised that our consumption of just one glass of beer each could make a difference to the apparent fit. Even more surprising was the discovery that it was not beer-linked – the pane of glass was indeed too small. The windows in the lounge and bedroom were to all intents and purposes identical but when we actually measured the separate panes they were slightly different sizes to those in the lounge, an eccentricity that could only happen in France. After an uncomfortable night in which the wind howled through the gaping window frames in our bedroom we paid a visit the next morning to the local *bricolage* to have two new panes of glass cut, in order to complete the job.

While browsing around the *bricolage* we were amazed at the low prices of ceramic wall tiles and showerheads, so cheap now the *livre* had recovered, certainly worth looking into in preparation for our next project – completing the bathroom. For a few years now we'd had to undergo the routine every spring of painting out the salt marks deposited on the lower half of the bathroom wall that built up over the winter months and appeared with amazing regularity each year. Now, we believed, was the time to do something about it, and upgrade the shower at the same time. We were becoming familiar visitors at the local *bricolage* and the proprietor now smiled at us and nodded in recognition. The next day we returned with our measurements, and bought the tiles, shower-head and shower rail.

We also made enquiries while we were there, about having a duplicate key cut for the kitchen door, which was one of those huge bevelled types peculiar to France. I'd visited about five sophisticated locksmiths in the UK to try to have a key cut;

each of them had peered at the key with interest and shaken his head. The helpful gentleman at the *bricolage* looked at the key and pointed out we needed to go no further than the *super-marché* across the road, and I looked puzzled. He pointed again at the supermarket opposite. I was certain I had not misunderstood him but whoever heard of supermarkets producing duplicate keys? Inside the supermarket there was no-one looking remotely like a locksmith so I had to inquire at the till. *"Demain matin,"* she repeated, leaving me even more perplexed. The next morning we returned yet again to the supermarket. Inside the foyer a gentleman was hard at work producing French car number plates and the customer was arguing with him over the number layout. Each time the numbers and spacings were slightly rearranged the customer was still not entirely happy. Eventually the gentleman left his rather obnoxious customer and came over to us. I produced the giant-sized key, that looked rather like a church door key than a household key and he took it, looking entirely comfortable with the request. He returned to the disgruntled customer, had a few words, disappeared into his little office at the back and five seconds later returned with a ready made exact duplicate, no cutting required. The gentleman was relieved to have such an easily satisfied customer, and we left with our goods feeling a little uneasy at the thought that our back door key was so readily available to all and at such a modest price! The two were still arguing as we left.

Our final purchases that day were a couple of new black dustbins with clip-on lids. For years we had been plagued with the continuing problem of refuse disposal. Visitors had instructions not to place bottles or any glass objects in black bags for the refuse collector. If the refuse man even suspected there were bottles in the refuse bags he would shake them to check for the familiar clink of glass. In the event of finding anything suspicious he would leave the bag by the side of the lane. Dustbins did walkabouts and visitors tended to leave mountains of black refuse bags and rows of bottles piled up in the garage on

Saturdays, for others to dispose of. In the hot summer months the smell of refuse throughout the cottage would become intolerable. If black bags were left at the side of the lane on Saturdays for the refuse collection on Tuesdays, within hours the local four-legged scavengers would have ripped open the bags and strewn refuse over an area of at least six square metres. Even the large wheely-bin belonging to *la grande maison blanche* had been tipped over on its side and the contents containing the remnants of their fish barbecue voraciously attacked one day, though no one ever saw the culprits at work. We hoped that by having bins with clip-on lids they could safely be left by the kitchen door on Saturdays and put out for collection on Tuesdays, hopefully partially solving the problem. Tilly painted our name on the bins and we hoped for the best on all fronts.

The poor old lavender bush in the herb bed was beginning to look a trifle sad. Although prolific still, it was becoming brittle and woody, spreading over the path and flattening with each downpour of rain. Other shrubs had begun growing through the middle of the bush and it looked decidedly untidy. One day I went into the garden with a saw and a pick-axe, hacked the thing mercilessly then attacked the roots with the pick-axe. Within half an hour the bush had gone and the whole appearance of the garden had altered dramatically. I couldn't believe the old lavender bush had taken up so much space. Finally, pining for the loss of the lavender bush as it once was, we planted a young, pot-grown variety to take its place.

One afternoon towards the end of our stay we were invited to Liz and Colin's house, which was situated in an isolated position on the outskirts of a pretty village, about a ten-minute drive from the cottage. The wooded lane leading to their house suddenly dipped quite steeply and a stone building came into view lying end-on to the right of the road, with an adjoining outbuilding which had been converted into a *gîte*. A large home-constructed *terrasse* ran across the front of the two buildings, and around the *gîtes* the land had been thoughtfully terraced and fell sharply away from the small garden into the most breathtaking view of a valley and distant hills beyond. Around the *terrasse* was a mass of brightly-coloured nasturtiums. The *gîtes* had all the usual characteristics that were typically Charentais, the thick stone walls, tiny shuttered windows and cool, dark interiors. The main *gîte* had an open plan living room with two or three central steps leading up to a balustraded kitchen area. Above the centrally situated kitchen table was suspended a large rectangular hanging-rack. A large wood-burning stove served the main area of the room, giving it a very cosy appearance. Liz pointed out that the three doors leading out of the room had all been painted different shades of medium blue, as she'd been unable to make up her mind which of the three colours to choose. She was therefore asking the opinions of various visitors before finally choosing one of the shades. The other parts of the house were still in the process of being converted and at that time a single precarious stepladder led up from the living room to the bedroom. So far most of their time and energy had gone into converting the adjoining *gîte*, which was let out in the summer and had doubled as their home in the winter. A lot of energy had gone into restoring the beautiful dark oak ceiling beams in the *gîte*, and an equally delightful dark stained staircase led up the side of the room to the bedrooms and shower room. We found the conversions and the surrounding countryside absolutely delightful, but could imagine it to be quite a lonely spot in the sometimes overcast, rainy winter months. We spent a relaxing evening at their house, before once more embarking on the long journey north.

At 'la grande maison blanche' a very large conifer plus a further tree had fallen on the side wall of the house, causing structural damage both inside and out.

CHAPTER NINE

CALM AFTER THE STORM

B etween Christmas and New Year, 1999, a fierce cyclone hit southwest France, bringing chaos and devastation to the region on a scale never known before. Winds of 120mph swept up the valley engulfing the area in widespread destruction. At Mortagne, a huge tidal wave swept through the harbour, wrecking boats and depositing them onshore, and flooding the entire area.

During the storm, which raged for over five hours, the barn sustained damage to three of its four roofs, leaving areas of ridge tiles jutting inward at awkward angles. A wooden rear wall of the garage, which was attached to the house, was demolished, opening up a previously unseen view from the house, of the countryside beyond.

At *la grande maison blanche* a very large conifer plus a further tree had fallen on to the side wall of the house, causing structural damage both inside and out. A crack appeared down the front wall of the house, adjacent to this end wall, as the large rectangular corner edging stones parted along the line of cement. As a result, the whole of the side wall of the house, which included the French windows, needed to be demolished and rebuilt. Electricity and telephone cables occupied a tangled mass across their front garden. The saddest loss was the complete devastation of the formal poplar wood and orchard. One hundred and fifty trees were either reduced to broken stubble or lay at dangerous angles, necessitating removal. A clear view of the house, which normally lay nestling in complete seclusion, could be seen from the lane beyond where the majestic poplar wood once lay, shielding the inmates of the house, and the occupants of the swimming pool. Apparently the storm swept up the valley, demolishing the poplar wood on its route, forming a rising vortex which passed above the three other houses occupying the centre of the hamlet, then sucked off the tiles of the high barn roof, which lay in its path.

By some unknown miracle, considering the cottage was situated in a very exposed position, our property was virtually untouched apart from damage to the television aerial, due mainly to the direction in which the cyclone had struck. Even the ancient pear tree, which spontaneously shed its branches of dead wood on to the lawn from time to time, surprisingly remained standing.

Cables littered the garden of the *gîte* behind ours, but the surrounding houses had largely protected the house itself. A fallen tree had narrowly missed causing structural damage to the house.

In the countryside around, lanes were impassable due to fallen trees. Three million homes, it was reported, were without electricity. In a matter of hours, the whole appearance of the countryside had changed, and the area had become completely paralysed. The electricity supply was cut off for the best part of a week, telephone lines were non-functional, trains could not run, computers crashed, banks were out of action, credit cards were dysfunctional and petrol purchase was limited to 100 *francs* worth of petrol per person. In such a situation, being a small farming community, everyone was anxious to help out their neighbours, and the community spirit was never more apparent. Builders, roofers and engineers were suddenly in desperate demand, doing their utmost to assess and repair the damage, most of them tirelessly working a fourteen-hour day. Insurance companies were not assessing damage under 15,000FF and were urging clients to quickly send in their claim forms. For those with substantial damage insurance companies were haggling, suppliers ran out of building and roofing materials, and manufacturers could no longer cope with demand. Only wood remained in plentiful, cheap supply.

Communication to and from the area had been exceedingly difficult. The English property owners in the hamlet were communicating with each other in the UK and discussing how best to help each other out. Eventually our American neighbour managed to reach a friend of his who lived in Saintes and who was in possession of a mobile phone. He very graciously volunteered to check the properties in the hamlet, in particular the big house, and was able to report back the news he was so hoping not to hear. Kevin, who'd been in England when the cyclone struck, returned to undertake the onerous task of removing the poplars one by one. This he attempted to accomplish at a rate of one tree per day until it was realised the task was too immense for a single person to undertake and he managed to get assistance.

Tom and Annabel made the journey to the Charente to see for themselves the state of their roof, and to attempt to make the house temporarily waterproof, with plastic sheeting, corrugated iron, strong tape, and sheer determination. In the meantime Monsieur Jaubert had written informing them of the state of their roof, a letter they did not receive until after they returned to the UK. Unfortunately they had at that stage employed a British builder to give them a quote for the work, out of sheer convenience of language communication. Four months later very little progress had been achieved. They had at last reached an agreement with the insurance company, who had argued that they were under-insured on the buildings side and insisted upon them paying the extra premium before they would allow their claim to be processed. The quote they had received from the British builder, obviously attempting to take advantage of the situation, was prohibitive and entirely unacceptable. Monsieur Jaubert had taken umbrage and refused to do the work unless they would allow him to re-tile the whole roof, an undertaking the insurance company, they were anxious to point out, would never agree to. Four months on, they had therefore turned full circle and were looking for another roofer who would be willing to undertake the enormous task of repairing their exceptionally high roof for a realistic sum.

When we eventually made the trip to the Charente and saw for ourselves the devastation that had occurred, we were quite

143

shocked. Whole groups of trees in what had been a very wooded area had either fallen or were lying at acute angles. Many isolated trees had been reduced to half their original size when huge trunks had broken off. Surprisingly it was the centre often of the wooded areas that had suffered the worst damage. This was not always evident until one walked into a wood, and viewed for oneself that the dense middle mass was actually tree after tree lying on top of one another, either entirely uprooted or lying at precarious angles to the ground.

Liz told us that immediately before the cyclone hit, with winds howling to a climax, she had attempted to walk down to her elderly neighbours' house to check that they were all right. She had walked out of the house and had advanced only a few metres when the wind became so forceful she could no longer move forward. All she could then do was to drop to the ground and wriggle slowly back to the house on her stomach, a terrifying experience. After the storm they went to check on their neighbours only to find a tree had fallen against the back door, another tree blocked the front door and they were trapped inside.

Colin possessed a barn that was in the midst of renovation. Helicopters taking television news pictures had flown over the disaster area, and zoomed in on the barn, taking pictures of poor Colin frantically waving his arms, indicating to them to go away as the draught from the helicopter was blowing the tiles off his brand new roof.

Five months after the disaster chain saws could still be heard felling and cutting up trees all day long at *la grande maison blanche*. Kevin showed us the house wall that needed to be demolished, held by wooden props, and bordering on to it, bare circles of earth in the grass, where the orchard had stood. A tree lying at a sixty-degree angle almost touching the pagoda, he pointed out, would also have to be removed. The grounds were unrecognisable minus the trees. The previous owners had been to view the damage and had for the second time in a small number of years, been reduced to tears.

Apparently poplars planted in rows had been specially vulnerable to storm damage, the theory being that roots normally spread out in all directions, but the roots of trees planted in rows compete with each other, upsetting the trees' balance when resisting fierce winds.

Tom and Annabel's roof was still covered in plastic sheeting; we were told the work couldn't be done until September. The remaining tiles would have to be removed as they were either chipped, had moved slightly out of position, or been weakened in some way. They had been back to Monsieur Jaubert but he would still not entertain tiling their roof, maintaining that the roof was too high and needed to be lowered, but this they felt, was also out of the question, due to cost. The tiles, which had been held on with lengths of wire, were Marseilles-type tiles and needed to be specially ordered. In the confusion they had forgotten to order the tiles, which, they were told, would take about two to three months. The new tiles, which would be screwed into position, would make the roof much more secure when eventually completed. Water had been leaking into the bedrooms and a musty damp smell was beginning to be apparent on the upper floor.

Kevin told us that roofers were demanding money up front, with no guarantee when the work would be done. Mostly, the tarpaulins had been removed and we spotted new roof patches on a large number of buildings around the area. Only ancient outbuildings and specialist roofs remained without roofs. Tractors had been used to help remove trees blocking roads and farmers were behind schedule with their work in the fields. Planting had started late. Sunflowers and maize seedlings were only just visible by late May. Everywhere was evidence of courage, determination and the beginning of a slow recovery.

At the cottage, the mains water tap had been replaced, thanks to Liz and Colin's persistence with the water authority, enabling the water to be isolated at last. Although it had taken half a dozen telephone calls, two aborted attempts on the part

145

of the engineer to find the house, and hours wasted waiting at the house for a workman to turn up, the official gas engineer finally arrived to fix the gas heater. It took him less than half an hour to change a water valve, fix the fault and disappear, leaving a bill for 740 francs. This time however, the water heater was left in reasonable working order, and in this respect it appeared to be money well spent.

The work in the *salle d'eau*, due to be undertaken between January and March, had necessarily taken low priority in the ensuing crisis following the storm. By mid-May we were still awaiting an estimate for the job, but we were promised a telephone estimate, and if we agreed, the work could go ahead the following week. By the time we arrived the old tiles in the shower unit had been removed and replaced with the modern beige and white tiles that we'd chosen the previous October. The modern shower unit was in place, minus the shower door, which had not yet been purchased. Kevin had commenced providing pine panelling over the lower two and a half feet of the walls, but had realised that panelling over suspect pipework could prove a disastrous move. He had therefore left untouched the wall leading up to the shower, and the toilet cubicle, until such time as a decision could be made on how best to complete the room. It was eventually decided that the rest of the wall should be tiled to the same height as the panelling, leaving the pipes exposed. This would unfortunately require the new tiles above the wash basin to be removed, in order to synchronise the basin tiles with the surrounding wall tiles once those in the shower area were linked up with those of the wash basin area and extended along the wall to the door-opening.

We again visited our favourite *bricolage* to order more tiles, but were told the warehouse at Orléans had burnt down and it would be two months before the tiles could be obtained from a further supplier. We were promised the tiles would be ready for us to collect when we returned in July. Looking on the bright side, at least we hadn't discovered that the very modestly priced tiles were end of range and unobtainable. Kevin told us that the tiler had had difficulty trying to make the tiles adhere to the gloss paint on the walls, and it had been necessary to burn the paint off before tiling over the painted areas. They had also found a leaking pipe beneath the bidet, causing a flood, necessitating a third repair in as many years. A plumber had been called to fix the pipe. The overall appearance of the *salle d'eau* at this point was pleasing, but it was impossible to ignore the burn marks on the wall adjacent to the pipe repair, also surrounding the shower area, and across the window of the shower. We decided it would help the tiler and give the room a temporary face-lift if we covered the remaining wall with a matt white emulsion, ready for the work to continue in the autumn. This we managed to complete during our time there. We rehung the shower curtain, to make the room acceptable for our summer visitors.

On this visit at least, we had not been greeted by nettles, weeds, an over-rambling rose and a lawn that was five feet tall. The surrounds to the cottage had been neatly strimmed, the lawn had been cut and the roses looked glorious. A honeysuckle had detached itself from the corner of the house wall and had formed a ludicrous low arch over the garden gate. The hedge had almost two feet of new growth. The roses covering the dry stone wall had grown over the path behind the herb bed, but the branches that had been trained over the metal tie by the rear kitchen door were profuse with white roses, veiling the metal tie magnificently. Happily the crack we'd cemented over, along the wedge-shaped stone above the kitchen door, remained closed and the kitchen door had not dropped further, but opened easily. We repainted the black iron garden gate, the hedge was dutifully trimmed and my back duly skinned performing the task, on our single day of hot sunshine, and the garden quickly returned to a semblance of neatness in a single morning. The garden however, had once again surrendered to the presence of moles, which were back in force and unhappily far more difficult to contain!

Rust had again appeared on the vents and lower edges of the blue metal shutters due to the constant winter downpours, and they had to be repainted. Parts of the kitchen wall and areas of the lounge around the open fireplace were looking shabby, so out came the paint pot once again. The jade cushions we'd brought along for the painted chairs were a perfect match. Little extras we'd bought such as a ceiling-hanging kitchen rack, spotlights for the *salle d'eau*, a kitchen clock, and a large framed sketch of the Dordogne, with a French inscription, found gathering dust in a charity shop in England, all took up their new places in the cottage. Newly acquired oak and brass bellows looked charming hung on the wall beside the open fireplace. We'd even bought a black iron Gothic plant-holder to enhance the outside wall of the *gîte*, complete with plants from the local market at Gémozac. At the end of an unusually rainy week we felt we'd achieved most of what we'd planned to achieve, including making an appointment with the *notaire's* office in order to belatedly pick up the deeds of the house. These had been held in their safe keeping for the last eight years, with little conscious effort on our part to retrieve them. The deeds were ready for us to sign for when we managed with some difficulty to find the *notaire's* office and the procedure was efficient and surprisingly painless.

The cottage was certain to be left in good order for the visitors who were to follow us in, although we had not been able to achieve success with the television aerial. The longest ladder in the hamlet was not quite long enough to reach the highest point of the roof, from where the aerial could be reached, and I could only leave a note for the visitors explaining why the television picture was not as clear as it should be. The people who would be staying at the cottage the week after we left were relatives of an elderly but naïve, kindly gentleman who had booked the cottage the previous year. He had been unable to take his holiday due to his wife's illness, and had failed to take out cancellation insurance although advised by us to do so. In the thirty years he had been taking holidays in France, he informed us, never once had he taken out cancellation insurance. The second week of his holiday he managed to pass on to his daughter and son-in law, but Liz, in the meantime, had made ready for absent visitors. A while after the absentees' holiday week, I received a telephone call from the son of the elderly gentleman. He informed me that the moment he realised his parents would be unable to take their holiday he had readvertised the holiday without success, and wondered if his father was entitled to have his money back. I pointed out that cancelling the holiday within a few days of departure unfortunately did not entitle him to be recompensed in this way because expenses had already been incurred. The caretaker had been paid for cleaning the cottage, and the gardener had spent two hours tidying the garden. The house could not be re-let at short notice, and his father had signed the Booking Conditions in which it was clearly stated under what conditions he would be allowed a refund. I didn't like to add salt to the wound in the circumstances, by pointing out that sub-letting on behalf of the client to strangers, was not ethical.

Weeks later I had a letter from the gentleman's daughter explaining that her mother was only just recovering from a fall, and her father had been in hospital, and generally was having a really bad time. She again asked if they could possibly be recompensed in some way. I opted to allow the elderly couple to retake their holiday free of charge the following year, when they had duly recovered from their various illnesses, and the daughter, in her reply, announced that her father was very happy with the idea. The arrangement was that I would write to them by Easter when I knew what weeks were free, to finalise the arrangements. I was therefore justifiably surprised when the gentleman rang me up shortly after Easter, thanking me for allocating them a holiday in June. Unfortunately he and his wife would not be able to take up the offer as they had just returned from France, but his daughter would love to take the opportunity to return there. I maintained that the arrangement had been made to benefit the people who had missed out on the holiday, namely the two of them, but failing to persuade the elderly gentleman, I eventually agreed that if that was his wish, his daughter could take up the holiday in his place. I did however, feel most uncomfortable about these arrangements.

We were completely unprepared when, a few days after the daughter and son-in-law returned from their holiday at the *gîte*, we received a letter full of strident remarks, with not one single positive comment to account for all our hard work. It had rained a lot, accompanied by high winds, and water had come in through the kitchen ceiling, which they had had to mop up. They had either not read or had ignored my note in the Information Folder explaining how water could occasionally blow underneath the Roman tiles in the event of sudden high winds but that did not necessarily mean the roof itself was leaking. A more helpful comment would have been to offer a report on the state of the roof over the area by the kitchen door through which the water was supposedly leaking. The roof was low enough at this point to be seen easily by some enterprising person merely climbing on to a chair. They complained that the electricity was unsafe, sparks were flying from the bathroom light switch, and the plug to the washing machine was not working. The most probable explanation for the latter, we felt, was that they had not read the attached instructions and had turned the start dial of the washing machine anti-clockwise to the start position instead of clockwise.

Fortunately we were in a position to confirm that none of these things had been faulty up to the day of their arrival, but would of course be looked in to. She ended the letter by stating the weather had been lousy, they had both caught colds, and the television was not working. Ironically, the temperature was 32 degrees C the day after they left, and remained scorching all week. We were slightly mystified as to why they had been so anxious to secure a second visit if they were not happy with the accommodation, especially as things had only changed for the better since their last visit.

Between this visit and our arrival in July, one other couple had stayed at the cottage. The pair had been taking short breaks in different areas of France, looking for a suitable property to buy. Between the time of booking and their arrival at the cottage however, the purchase of their dream home in France had already materialised, and the need to spend a superfluous week in the Charente-Maritime was obviously irritating them. During Liz's post-arrival visit they were brimming with enthusiasm over the property they had just bought in Bergerac, which was exactly what they wanted. She gathered from various snippets of conversation that they really hadn't wanted to take the cottage holiday. All their thoughts were on the house in Bergerac, but they realised they would not get their money back at short notice. Liz's impression was that they were "dripping with money," owning a particularly expensive sports car with personalised number plates. Unfortunately, good weather had rather eluded them and this was something they were unable to purchase. They were plagued with bad weather throughout and had disappeared for three days during their stay. The key was returned promptly, together with a comment about leaving the bed linen out for Liz, as they had not wanted to use the washing machine on the last day. We'd asked Liz not to bother to clean up after them, as we would be following them in.

Although we were rather surprised to find barbecue ash dumped in the back lane when we arrived, and had to deal with a bin full of rubbish and rotting food that had not been bagged, the house was reasonably tidy and I returned the lady's security deposit immediately.

We could find no problem at all with the electricity, no sparks from the switches, and the washing machine, as we expected, was in perfect working order.

As always, although it was our holiday, we spent a good deal of time finding tasks to do. We'd brought along four expensive border tiles in deep pink and beige, that we'd managed to acquire end of range, to edge the new tiles over the wash basin, and eliminate the need to remove these tiles as first thought necessary. The tiles, when fixed in place, looked extremely effective. We replaced the pine towel rails, tooth mug and soap holders that had been removed for redecoration and Tilly took it upon herself to varnish the new wall panelling. The extra tiles we'd ordered in May however, had failed to materialise by the end of our holiday and we were beginning to feel that our favourite *bricolage* was rapidly becoming our former favourite.

On the second day of our holiday we all three rushed off to the hospital at Saintes after Keith failed to follow the most fundamental rule of using a sharp knife and accidentally sliced deeply into the ball of his thumb whilst trimming a home-made clothes-prop. He left the hospital with six stitches in his thumb and lucky to still have a thumb intact. The treatment he received during the subsequent four visits to the hospital was second to none, in spite of the doctor's unreserved shrieks of *'mon dieu!'* a far cry from a typical British reaction perhaps, of 'Oh yes, very nasty!' on viewing the state of the traumatised thumb with the bandages removed. This had the subsequent effect of shattering the little remaining confidence Keith possessed that his thumb would ever regain a state of normality. Certainly, swimming and heavy or intricate jobs around the house were in the short term quite definitely suspended. The week certainly served to intensify our somewhat sparse knowledge of French medical terminology. We were not aware of it at the time, but Colin had also been admitted to the hospital, having suffered a stroke a month earlier. He had been readmitted for further tests around the time of our visit, which accounted for the fact that we had not been able to contact Liz by phone. When we eventually caught up with her, Colin was recovering well, and about to be discharged from hospital.

It was now essentially up to me to take on the burdensome tasks of completing the inside of the ground floor shutters with a coat of blue paint, and climbing to the very top of the ladder to repaint the side wall of the house, using the roller extension. An unenviable task by all accounts, and one I did not relish.

The side wall of *la grande maison blanche* however, had some-how escaped its considered demise. In July scaffolding had been erected in front of the house and two workmen, one French, one English, were brilliantly expounding Anglo-French cooperation into an effective and quite miraculous repair. Intricate ornate work beneath the eaves had greatly enhanced the appearance of the house. The exterior of the house had been repainted, and apart from a hiatus created by the loss of the desired seclusion, it looked splendid.

Our seclusion had been further enhanced by ten inches of growth on the privet hedge since I'd last hacked it at the beginning of June, and the purchase of a trumpet vine, or *trompets de Jericho* as the shrub is affectionately known by the local people. The shrub would hopefully, according to plan, spread rapidly over and along the fence to create a prolifera-tion of bright orange trumpet-like flowers during the summer months.

I was anxious, during our stay, to replace the bed-settee, which we had been reluctant initially to dispose of because it made an exceptionally firm bed. The sight of the ancient piece of furniture as a permanent fixture in the downstairs bedroom however, was becoming an eye-sore, and certainly not ideal beneath a mattress that overhung the bed-settee by two inches on either side. In a furniture store in Royan we spotted what appeared to be a very modestly priced pine bed, until we realised that in France the bed frame and the base are priced and sold separately. A sensible idea, considering the bed base wears to a greater degree than the frame and can be replaced eventually. We bought the bed and arranged for it to be deliv-ered free of charge to the cottage three days later. Not only did the delivery men find the house with no problem at all but the bed, which was delivered flat packed, was carefully bolted together, checked and placed in position in the bedroom. For a small charge, we had arranged for the bed-settee to be taken away and the two men lightheartedly heaved the incredibly heavy piece of furniture into the van, refusing all offers of help, and drove away, having left us a spare bolt and two Allen keys into the bargain. A few days later we bought a flat-packed pine bedside table, again very reasonably priced, to enhance the effect of our new bed. No longer was it necessary to balance ourselves over a convex mattress, and risk marking the chair linen with our early morning cup of coffee.

On our final day at Le Petit Hameau the gas-heater began to play up yet again. This time the replaced gas valve seemed to be reluctant to close and the heater appeared to be trying to re-ignite after the water had been turned off, causing the inevitable slight smell of gas. There seemed to be very little we could do apart from leave a note to the family following us in, and hope the problem would rectify itself, without Liz having to call the gas engineer back yet again.

Our return journey was to be broken by a stay in the Limousin region. Here the familiar fields of sunflowers, maize and vines of the Charente-Maritime, suddenly gave way to narrow lanes, green fields and high hedges, rather like the England of many years ago without the traffic congestion and over-population. Essentially a cattle-rearing area, it was a stark contrast to the *département* we'd just left. Houses were built on granite, with none of the underlying damp problems of our area. We noticed that very few of the older houses had iron ties on the walls, or cracks appearing along walls, resulting from subsidence. We stayed in a tiny *gîte*, which had a steeply slop-ing roof with dormer windows and a rough granite floor. A simple wooden open staircase led to two bedrooms with untreated floorboards and sloping beams running from floor to ceiling. The floor slightly tilted in places, and between the floorboards were gaps, huge by ordinary standards, allowing the upper floor to be weirdly illuminated by the light down-stairs. One of the floorboards in our bedroom sported a miss-ing knot in the wood through which Tilly would poke her slen-der fingers the moment she heard us stir in the morning. There were no curtains, no ceiling lampshades, and floor coverings were practically non-existent. Everything had been kept very simple and the tiny house was very easy to keep clean. Although it made our cottage seem enormous, rambling and over-equipped, we found the place quaint and cosy, in spite of the small basketwork three piece suite, which had ridges that seemed to prod into our rib cages in a most uncomfortable fashion. We could appreciate what the owners, a friendly, helpful hard-working English couple, were trying to achieve. The husband was a builder. They told us they had advertised a *gîte* and two studios, then waited with baited breath to see what the response was before starting the restorations. They had received no response at all for the studios, so they hadn't bothered to convert them. He had however, installed a gas water-heater in the *gîte* that was far superior to ours, with automatic electronic ignition and a balanced flue, and we resolved to investigate the possibility of replacing our troublesome water-heater with such a sophisticated model during our next visit to *Le Petit Hameau*.

Tilly greatly appreciated the *gîte* owners' six dogs and three horses. We didn't mind the curtained off food cupboard with the curtain that wouldn't budge on the curtain rod, and the shower that was open on two sides. We watched the gentleman up the lane refusing to pick his runner beans, which positively drooled over his wire fence into the lane, inviting surreptitious pickings by various passers-by, while our *gîte* owner explained that *Monsieur* only grew them for the orange flowers. Everyone in the little village seemed to own a dog, and our progress on the occasional evening stroll through the village could be monitored by a procession of dog barks, followed by advances from various owners, who greeted us with understanding smiles and cheerful '*bonsoirée*'s.

A holiday stroll that proved to be rather more than we bargained for was an occasion in which we parked the car at the *Sentier de Randonnée* at four o'clock one hot afternoon to follow the one and a half hour red route stroll marked on the map there. The beautiful walk through the woods and by the stream continued along a ravine and past the ruins of the ancient town. Still following the red signs marked on the trees, we passed down a country lane, through more woods, farmyards, and fields. We climbed over fallen trees, waded through thick mud, continuing to follow the signs, until we began to believe we were either extremely slow walkers or someone was playing a practical joke and had altered the route. Four hours later, after passing along a wooded lakeside, with the red signs still visible, we came at last upon a place we recognised, and realised for certain that we were on the wrong route. We were miles from the car, miles from the *gîte*, we had no money, no mobile telephone, no food or drink, the light was beginning to fade, and we were becoming increasingly exhausted. At length we decided to make for the nearest small town, which was three kilometres down a deserted lane, and seek help. After what seemed the longest three kilometres imaginable, we hobbled with the aid of sticks, into the Town Square, and sank exhausted on to wooden seats in the centre of the Square. Opposite was a bar and we spotted a young man through the open window, busy tidying tables. We hobbled over to the window and attempted in crude French, to explain our predicament. A young lady came over to the window, spoke to us, then to the young gentleman, who immediately grabbed his car keys, took us over to his car, and drove us the eight kilometres back to our car, at the *Sentier de Randonnée*. We were so grateful to the anonymous French gentleman who gave us the lift we practically fell over ourselves thanking him. Our *gîte* owners were so alarmed on being told of our unfortunate experience that they resolved to have a word with the *Mairie* concerning the lack of clear directions, which could have led to even more serious consequences.

An English couple we met in the Limousin had spent a week searching for a home to buy in a price range of between £9-14,000. They were not having an awful lot of luck, until about the last day of our stay, when they had at last found something they could almost afford and were about to put in an offer. Another enterprising English couple we met had moved out to the Limousin in June, bought a house that was little more than a shell, and had rented a small caravan until the place could be made habitable. They had settled in to country life with their three dogs and a rather rotund, black, spiky but adored pet pig, and were hoping to either purchase enough adjoining land to keep five hundred sheep, or restore and sell their existing house in order to acquire a farmhouse with more land. They had already had a shower and toilet installed, and were hoping to have central heating installed before the weather broke, and be able to move into the main house. An excellent plumber lived in the village nearby, but they had been warned to catch him early in the day before he'd had chance to uncork a bottle. The few English people we met in the Limousin had the same characteristics in common, determination to succeed and be accepted into the French community, and an ability to enjoy the simple life of the French countryside.

A shock awaited us on our arrival back in the UK, in the form of a letter full of scathing criticisms written by the lady who had just bought a house in the Bergerac area of France. Now that her security deposit had been safely banked, she wrote, she felt free to speak her mind. They had not wanted to trouble Liz when she had visited them on arrival after her disclosure that her husband had been taken into hospital, but they had never stayed in a house that was so filthy. They had to put up with their feet sticking to the floors, which she maintained, had not been cleaned for a very long time. The kitchen was a health hazard. There were remains of other peoples' food on the crockery. They had preferred to barbecue under their umbrellas in order to avoid using the cooker or the microwave, and had stayed in the cottage for only four nights. She had even compared our three bed-roomed detached cottage for six, situated within half an hour of sandy beaches, to a two-bedroomed farmhouse for four, with outbuildings and no garden that they'd previously rented in the Central Massif. She described the latter as being twice the value for three-quarters of the price. Obviously booking such a large house had proved expensive for just two people. We calculated that the price per person for the stated number of people per week was actually cheaper staying at our *gîte*, regardless of position. The letter was full of the most disparaging remarks we had ever received. It would have upset Liz, one of the most conscientious workers we had yet encountered. I'm sure she would have preferred the couple to have had a gentle word with her at the time if they felt so strongly about the state of the cottage, than hear cowardly complaints in writing weeks afterwards. At least she would have been given the chance to examine the causes of complaint and if necessary put things right.

Had it not been for the fact that we had followed her in to the cottage, something she could not have known about, and were in a position to either dispute such allegations, or dismiss them as grossly exaggerated accounts of minor legitimacy, we would have been very upset indeed. Having been on site however, and having worked so hard at the beginning of the season, washing paintwork, crockery and linen, redecorating the *salle d'eau*, and generally cleaning up the cottage for our summer visitors, we felt deeply hurt and dispirited by the criticisms that were obviously designed to upset. I felt anger over her implications that she felt her security deposit would be at risk if she said nasty things about the cottage, and having waited so long before feeling obliged to make such claims. We reflected upon the state of the cottage upon our arrival. The cooker had been clean. The house certainly had not been 'filthy', and not for one instant had our feet stuck to the floor. Our only complaint on arrival was that the crockery drainer I'd spent twenty minutes cleaning in May could have done with another thorough clean, and a water mark had appeared on the wall where the roof had leaked in June, and needed a spot of paint. That would probably have been enough for an enterprising person to set in motion a string of unjustified complaints, especially if she had been given the briefest hint that a couple had just taken a complimentary holiday in the cottage, and they themselves had really not wanted to be there. We had been warned about 'professional complainants', people making unjustified complaints, usually when the weather had been poor, in order to secure compensation, or even for the thrill of causing trouble. The complaints are never immediate, are never substantiated by photographic evidence or a third party, and usually have inconsistencies that combine to nullify them.

There were certainly inconsistencies in the lady's story. She had stated they only stayed in the place for four days, which meant they would have left on the Thursday morning, as they could not 'tolerate' it any longer. She had also stated that they had not been there to put the dustbin out, yet dustbin day was a Tuesday. Our calculations were borne out by Kevin's remark that our visitors had disappeared for three days, and returned later in the week. It seemed strange too, that someone could believe that a barbecue had the edge on the cooker or microwave in terms of cleanliness, and they would prefer to stand out in the rain barbecuing. Even stranger was the fact that she had gone on to state that the lounge, the ground floor bedroom and the bathroom were 'cleanish', and it was lovely to have a comfortable *salon.* Fortunately the two other families staying at the cottage had both enjoyed wonderful holidays.

The genuine gloom and disillusionment however, that we inevitably suffered after reading such letters of complaint, often lingered in our minds for many days, prompting various forms of post-mortem examinations, but was something, as property owners, we had been very gradually coming to terms and learning to cope with. One learns to be able to distinguish genuine complaints. Often in certain circumstances the people who should complain frequently fail to. One also learns to establish standards of cleanliness, work within those perimeters, and ignore those imposed upon one by mischief-makers, disappointed with the weather. Feelings do not always respond to logic and reasoning however, and this time I felt we'd been dealt a knock-out blow. For the first time I found myself taking it personally, and having grave misgivings about my capacity as a *gîte* owner.

CHAPTER TEN

ON EVEN GROUND

With these feelings still uppermost in our minds, and our grim faces reflecting the even gloomier weather, we set off for our autumn visit to Le Petit Hameau, at the October half term. We arrived at the Shuttle with an hour to spare, to be told that the train for which we had reservations was full, and we would be put on the next available train. This was somewhat of a blow as we'd planned to push quickly on to Orléans in time to pick up an electronically igniting gas water heater from the GME store before it closed at 18.00 hours. The store was the only one on our route with a Saturday opening that appeared reachable before closing time. Liz had arranged for a heating engineer to call at the cottage on the Tuesday, with a view to fitting the apparatus. Further delays due to closure of the tunnel on the Rouen by-pass saw the chance of our reaching Orléans in time slipping away rapidly, as a *deviation* sent us crawling through the centre of Rouen, with a distinct lack of directions on how to get back on to our original route again. Unexpected progress however, on a new dual carriageway beyond Rouen meant there was still a realistic possibility that we might reach our destination before the store closed, but our hearts sank as thick traffic on the approach to Orléans slowed us down to a crawl yet again, with an alarming twenty-five minutes remaining before closing time. It was indeed fortunate that since picking up a magazine with the listed opening times in one of their stores eighteen months earlier, they had extended the Saturday opening time to 19.00 hours.

We knew the store stocked the gas water-heater, but those on display bore little resemblance to the one we'd used in the Limousin. A numbered queuing system at the sales advice counter meant another half-hour delay, before eventually determining that they had such a water-heater in stock. We duly paid over the money, and were indicated over to the collection point to pick up our goods. Here, there was yet another ridiculous delay, as the person manning the desk eyed us suspiciously but appeared not to want to serve us, or take our paperwork. He chatted to a Frenchman who appeared to be adding infinite extra items of purchase to his already mountainous pile of goods, and our vacuous gentleman at the desk just tapped away furiously at his computer, ignoring us. Finally the gentleman who had served us originally came rushing up to us with an embarrassed smile and tried to explain that although the computer had told him there was an apparatus in stock there had been a fault in the updating and in fact there wasn't one after all. Before I could comprehend quite what was happening he began counting out the money I'd paid him using my Visa card and apologetically pushed a pile of francs into my hand. We could try the store in Bordeaux, he explained, or try the big store two kilometres further down the road, which also sold the gas water heaters. Happily we found the alternative store. They happened to sell a different brand of gas water heater. The lady who served us systematically searched her computer for an apparatus of the correct power and gas supply. She looked pleased when she managed to come up with the exact requirements, only to then deflate us with the news that the apparatus had to be ordered and could be collected in twelve days' time. In all we had spent three frustrating and fruitless hours in Orléans, before continuing on in worsening weather, with pouring rain and pockets of thick fog, for the remaining three-hour journey to the Charente-Maritime.

Apart from mouse droppings on both of the single beds, and one of the pillows I'd recently bought unfortunately displaying a mouse-hole with further droppings and pillow contents scattered over the bed, the *gîte* seemed largely as we had left it a few weeks earlier. By some profound miracle and with utter incredulity we turned on the dreaded water heater to find it functioning normally. There was no smell of gas as the main flame tried to re-ignite itself, with the associated popping sound after the water was turned off. There had been no apparent concerns or pertinent questions asked over the state of the water heater. There need be no trip to Bordeaux after all. For the time being the equipment had won a temporary reprieve.

The following morning we opened up the shutters on to bright

161

sunshine and a total absence of the expected autumn chill. Even the leaves on the Virginia creeper had not yet reached their shades of autumn bronze and red, and the breathtaking stillness of the rural view from the window was broken only by occasional bird-song. It was quite extraordinary that the combination of sunshine and the distinctive ambience at the cottage, even after eight years, could still work its magic charm and cause us to relax and com-pletely unwind, even given extreme circumstances.

We wandered out into the garden and peered over towards the barn, and its new roof, which had been scheduled for completion in September. We were astonished to see the plastic covering still in place and the work not done. We could hear Annabel's familiar voice, which surprised us, as she usually had to work during the half-term period. The builder apparently, was still awaiting arrival of the Marseilles tiles. Their visit materialised after Kevin had checked that the waterproof covering to their roof was hold-ing after days of heavy rain, only to find the ceiling of one of the upstairs bedrooms had caved in, and the ceiling of their new shower room appeared to be damp and rather suspect. Annabel, her sister and daughter had all flown down to Bordeaux to deal with the crisis, leaving their men folk holding the fort at home. All day they had been carrying mattresses downstairs, burning log fires to dry out the place, and collecting supplies of logs from the grounds of *la grande maison blanche*, having been invited to help themselves from their huge stockpile of redundant wood. The builder had been summoned to explain why the tarpaulins had been removed and to advise on the current position. It was a dire situation for them all, but one they were well used to, and one in which, as always, they were coping beautifully.

The owners of the *gîte* behind ours were also visiting for an autumn break, and like us, revelling in the beautiful autumn weather. The tiny mimosa sapling I'd pulled out of the lawn and given to them two or three years previously was now a flourish-ing three feet high shrub. Occasionally they would punish with secateurs the potent ivy that was nevertheless boldly beginning to take hold along the main trunk of the apple tree. They were presently trying to do battle with the persistent bamboo they had cleared from the area before having their new drive built, but which still regularly invaded the drive. Their four-year saga of the blocked loo, which had defeated plumber after plumber, each placing rods down the loo and trying various other potential solutions, had at last, they were delighted to report, been successfully remedied. They explained that when they had had their *fosse etranche* replaced with a new *fosse septique* the workmen had inadvertently severed the pipe leading from the loo. Only when Monsieur Jaubert, the local *maçon*, was summoned, was the problem solved. Using a high-pressure water pump through the toilet, a water fountain had appeared to suddenly grace the middle of their garden, at the site of the severed pipe. They had then dug a hole, found the suspect pipe, which was then carefully linked up to its less offensive destination with one inch of spare pipe in hand, and one family at least were very relieved.

Over at the back of the hamlet, the outside of the cottage owned by the French couple was receiving meticulous attention. Work had begun slowly chipping off the old outside wall facing, sandblasting and refacing the surface of the house. The industrious couple had taken it upon themselves to do the work involved and the effect looked very promising, although progress was slow, as the owner worked away from home during the week and had little time to commit himself to such intricate, time-consuming enterprises.

The haystack that had for a number of years screened any view of the distant woods that residents of the barn might have enjoyed, had at last been demolished at the end of harvesting. Loss of their immediate habitat probably accounted for the early visits by our furry friends. So too, did the swarm of red beetles mourn their loss when I performed my autumn hacking of the rose in front of the cottage. Two days later they had left their prickly abode and had gathered in earnest – or I should say in clusters – at the corners of the inset garage doors and could not be persuaded to leave their ill-chosen new home, even with the assistance of a broom.

A disturbing discovery was that the crack above the kitchen door, in spite of weeks of rain, appeared to have opened up again slightly, inside and out, which gave grounds to our theory that the tie was not the whole answer to the problem. We should have perhaps considered having the lintel above the kitchen door replaced at the same time. We would have to wait and see. Good news at last on discovering the tiles for the *salle d'eau* had arrived at last, and Kevin had been able to collect them.

The most refreshingly invigorating news was recorded in the Visitors' Book. Both families staying at the cottage had greatly enthused about their holidays there. After the intense disappointment of remarks made earlier in the year, it was wonderful to read their comments. The little boy had written, "It is really good in this house. We have had a wonderful time." Other comments followed. "This has been the perfect base for a memorable family holiday in this beautiful area of France. Thank you." The gentleman had written, "This has been, without a doubt, one of the best holidays ever. The weather was great, the area is lovely, especially Plage des Vergnes, and you have made it all possible. We are extremely grateful to you for allowing us into your French home, which has all, and more than one would expect from a *gîte*." In the wake of those comments, all our traumas, the frustrations, the disappointments, any resentment over the hard work involved, suddenly melted away in a newfound euphoria. We felt we should be thanking them for igniting in us a renewed sense of purpose and plenitude.

Our revised plan now was to take advantage of the strong pound, take the bull by the horns and push ahead with our programme of replacements, and try to finish most of the remaining work on the house, in a grand effort to make the *gîte* a place people would want to visit and revisit.

Our first intention was to replace the refrigerator whilst we were there. The one presently in use belonged originally to the previous owners. It was old; the plastic had cracked in a couple of places. Rust was beginning to appear around the edges and it had suffered badly in the flow of water resulting from the burst pipe in the wall. Above all it was too small for a family of six living in a country area, ten minutes by car from the nearest supermarket, with no village shop in the immediate vicinity. Our dilemma was how to make the best use of space. We decided to buy a small under-bench fridge to replace the present one, and in addition, a larger fridge-freezer that would be housed by the kitchen door, for use by larger families, the two were to be delivered the afternoon prior to our day of departure.

A further priority was to cancel the Tuesday visit of the gas-heating engineer, which involved driving into Gémozac and eating a rather large slice of humble pie. That done we diverted our attention to the provision of a shower door, to avoid visitors flooding the floor of the *salle d'eau* each time someone took a shower. This undertaking proved to be not in the least straightforward, as the width of the shower was at least fifteen centimetres above the standard size and there were water pipes running across the base of the wall on to which the door would have to be attached. It seemed that there was only one door that would fit our requirements, and it was not an inward opening or folding door, but a pivot-type door, opening outwards. We would therefore have to determine whether the door would open sufficiently to be able to step inside without the door hitting the side of the bidet. This could not be assessed easily without seeing one of the doors, and such non-standard doors were usually only available on order. For the time being, until it could be studied in a little more depth, the door would have to be put on hold and a curtain would have to suffice.

Arrangements to upgrade the inside of the garage roof were our next priority after completion of the tiling in the *salle d'eau*. Daylight could be seen from the inside of the garage roof, and all that existed between nature and us were gaping wooden boards and arched tiles. Although the roof was very high, the beams needed to be treated and the areas between the beams required insulating and plasterboarding. Hopefully people would no longer need to make an uncomfortable dash from the upstairs bedrooms through the cold and cobwebs to visit the *salle d'eau* and toilet. At the same time the two unsightly, cemented up small windows in the garage could be re-established, providing more light and removing the slightly derelict appearance that existed at that corner of the house. To provide windows where once they had existed required planning permission from the Mairie, and this would have to be sought, and could delay the work somewhat. Kevin's friend, a builder, would be over to assess the work involved in mid November.

Over lunch on the patio we discussed with Liz the various happenings in the small farming community, and our projects to be completed over the coming months. Colin was doing well and was back at work. Ros, it was rumoured, had left the flat and its inexorable and burdensome memories behind, and was living with a friend in relative obscurity, visiting her two sons and attempting to get her life back together again. Although we no longer were in contact with her, our thoughts were often with her, and we so wished her situation could be mitigated in some way.

Liz had kindly arranged for a television engineer to visit the following day to fix the television at last. I showed her the tiny blue lampshade I'd made for the little walnut lamp I'd picked up earlier at the antique shop in Boutenac-Touvent for eighty francs. The newly renovated lamp looked very sweet. I told her of my plans to make life easier for her by replacing the silver-grey washing-up bowl and dish-rack, which had taken me twenty minutes to clean in the summer, with a more practical bottle-green wire rack and bowl. Liz had a few reservations about the idea and hinted that the water was so full of calcium that marks would adhere to them anyway. She eventually left carrying a bunch of French onions, a piece of vintage cheddar and a couple of tiny new mimosa saplings we'd removed from the lawn.

Although we waited in all day the following day, the TV engineer did not arrive. After breakfast I'd made an early start by painting the now yellowing skirting board in the *salon* a crisp white. The white distemper-covered plaster boarding covering the walls in the lounge would soon need a coat of paint. We'd made the mistake once before, of attempting to cover distemper with emulsion, with disastrous peeling effects. The walls would obviously have to be treated first. Later we busied ourselves touching up the tiny blue upstairs shutters where rust was just visible along the lines of the metal studs, repainting black metal ties, strimming round the edge of the cottage and various stone tubs, and generally taking advantage of the beautiful weather. Although French workmen often work well into the evening, as the light began to fail it was obvious that the engineer would not be coming.

We had one day left at the cottage before returning to the UK, during which we'd made arrangements for the *fosse* to be cleared, and the fridges to be delivered. I naturally found myself plagued with doubt as to whether or not our previous day's experience would be replicated, and speculating on the problems we would face if they didn't turn up. Just before dawn the next day we breathed a sigh of relief as the familiar sound of the lighted heavy tanker could be heard backing alongside the garage door, and a dear little man, with a red beret pulled well down over his forehead to combat the early morning mist and drizzle, grinned and nodded knowingly towards the two *fosse* openings. It was especially thrilling for me to watch the man for the first time successfully utilising the hook I'd embedded in the concrete surface of the homemade *fosse* lid.

By 17.00 hours that afternoon, there was still no sign of the fridges, which according to the salesman, would be delivered at *midi*. Panic was beginning to take hold once again, as alternative arrangements were out of the question. I rang the shop at 17.30 hours, trying to keep my French conversation down to simple sentences such as *"Où sont nos livraisons?"* They assured me the goods would be delivered that day. My worry was that if the light began to fail they would not be able to find the cottage. An hour later the van pulled up outside and we relaxed. The delivery man explained that the contents would have to settle and we could not switch them on until the following morning.

Packing up linen and closing down for the winter, in addition to checking fridges, can be more time-consuming than anticipated. As we were locking the final shutters and about to leave the cottage, conscious of the fact that we were more than an hour late, a van drew up to the door. It was the television engineer. He gave a perfunctory shrug, unconcerned, when I suggested he was a little later than the expected *mercredi*. There was no knowing when the opportunity of fixing the television would arise again if we sent him away. I asked if it could be done quickly as we were late for *le shuttle*. He quickly lifted his tall ladder off the van, walked round into the garden, and propped the ladder against the wall. In the space of three minutes he had climbed the ladder, walked precariously up the steepest part of the roof to the chimney stack, loosened the base of the aerial, turned it round, secured it,

He climbed the ladder, walked precariously up the steepest part of the roof to the chimney stack, loosened the base of the aerial, turned it round, secured it, returned to his van and wrote out a bill...

returned to his van and written out a *facture* for 277 francs. Our neighbour, who had also had damage to his aerial after the cyclone, had bravely decided to fix it himself, by climbing on to his lean-to veranda, and from there on to the more gently sloping main roof. In a comical two-way conversation through the chimney to his wife below, he directed the aerial round until a correct picture appeared on all channels, and saved himself the expense of calling out a television engineer. Anyway, our television picture was returned to normal, as with the refrigerators, too late for us to benefit on this occasion, and at last we were on our way.

Journeying to the UK was usually a time for reflection and speculation on the home we were leaving behind. We always ventured a long lingering look at the cottage as we left, pondering on the number of intervening months before we could return again, and whether we'd absent-mindedly left any underwear on the washing line likely to be embarrassingly viewed throughout the winter months by all and anyone using the lane. We always hated leaving the cottage; it looked so lonely shuttered up. Le Petit Hameau came to life during the summer months, when every house was occupied. The local farmers smiled and waved when they noticed the shutters and windows of our *gîte* open. We felt so much a part of the community we were leaving behind following our relatively short stays, that the wrench seemed enormous.

On this particular journey, there was plenty of time for reflection. Two forty-minute hold-ups, due to major road works, followed by two further hold-ups caused by road accidents, extended our journey time by an unfortunate two hours. On the whole though, traffic delays permitting, the journeys were becoming easier. New motorways now ran directly south from Calais to Rouen, which meant it was no longer necessary to skirt Paris and travel on the dreaded and often lethal *peripherique* with high-speed traffic constantly zigzagging from lane to lane. More motorways were under construction, which would make the route south even more straightforward in future. There were now cheap flights to Bordeaux, and the TGV (*trains à grande vitesse*) or high-speed train could take you to Angoulême, both about an hour away. These were certainly worth investigating for such times when we could envisage just the two of us travelling. We no longer felt obliged to cram the car full of items of furniture and incidentals; with the strong pound most items were now cheaper to buy in France.

We had been rather put off the idea several years ago of buying a trailer for the car, in order to transport extra large items down to France. Keith's friend, who owned a house in the south of France, had set off one morning towards Dover, complete with trailer. Just a few miles into his journey, at the point where the road divided into two motorways, on checking his wing mirror he was amazed to see sparks flying and then to find himself being overtaken by a solitary wheel, merrily finding its own way along the motorway. Seconds later it became unmistakably apparent that the runaway wheel was his wheel that had detached itself from the trailer, with unforeseen consequences. The wheel hit a central bollard, flew up in the air, then shot off at speed along the wrong motorway and was never seen again by its astonished owner, the incident thwarting his journey somewhat. Fortunately the event occurred in the early hours of the morning, with little traffic about.

We had to bear in mind when assessing whether to purchase a trailer however, that such incidents were common occurrences in the life of his ill-fated friend, who lived in an elegant house in a crime-ridden suburb of London in which thefts were rife and home security was an utmost priority. He'd once owned a caravan, which unfortunately he'd been obliged to park in the road in front of his house, taking the precaution always to wedge the caravan tightly between two parked cars, one being his own. He looked out one morning and was amazed to find the two parked cars still in the same position but the caravan had disappeared. Months later, after official searches had refused to reveal its whereabouts, and after collecting the insurance money, the Irish police phoned with the unwelcome news that the stolen caravan had been found in Ireland, and would be duly returned to its reluctant owner. Shortly afterwards the police rang again with an unexpected development to the episode. On the return journey they had amazingly driven under a low bridge and unwittingly taken the roof off the caravan! Not surprisingly, our enthusiasm never stretched to buying a trailer.

Tilly was now sixteen and a talented flautist, performing with the top touring concert band in our local vicinity, a world away from French rural living. The flute, and sometimes the keyboard, always came on holiday with us, and even in the relative isolation of the French countryside, neighbours reacted kindly to the sound of her practising, occasionally with her father accompanying her on the keyboard. There might not be many more times when she would want to come on holiday with us. Soon she would want her own friends around her. She had developed a taste for French cheeses, especially *fromage de chèvre* and St Paulin, and sulked when I explained that back home we could not continue the French tradition of a cheese course before dessert.

In spite of voracious consumption of French cheese and wine when we visited the cottage, I was curiously surprised and delighted that having suffered frequent bouts of migraine, which had dogged me since the birth of my daughter, these never once occurred on any visit to our home in France. It was something I could never quite understand. On this occasion, however, we had been completely caught out by the unseasonably warm October/November weather; we had endured the misery of suffering enormous and frequent mosquito bites, and had of course neglected to include any preventative or calming lotion.

We reflected on the time we had brought my eighty-five year old father-in-law with us to the cottage for a holiday one May. The car had been heavily laden with a double futon, the mattress composed of extremely heavy layered-cotton. It had taken three people to lift the mattress on to the roof rack. We were so over laden that the automatic cruise control could not cope on the motorway inclines and the car lost speed dramatically on each uphill run. Keith's father however, so enjoyed the journey that his habit of dozing off each day for eighteen of the twenty-four hours, oblivious to his immediate surroundings, deserted him completely and he managed to quietly relish the dramatic changes of scenery and building style that could be observed along the route. The weather was warm for the time of year, and grandpa would sit out on the patio, clothed in his two sweaters and white sun hat with the brim turned down, enjoying his glass of wine and putting the world to rights. Occasionally he could be persuaded to walk with Tilly down the lane as far as the little bridge over the stream, and enjoyed visits to the cathedral and Roman amphitheatre at Saintes, and a cognac distillery that was part of an old *château*, even a stroll around the hollyhock-decked Talmont. He certainly would not have missed the opportunity to visit for the world, although initially, hampered by a pre-conception of a long, tiring, uncomfortable journey, followed by having to suffer blistering intolerable heat, strange food and with an intuitive feeling that he would be happier staying at home, he'd taken some persuading.

The fun of owning one's own *gîte* of course, is that at times when the weather perhaps is not so good, one can acquire as much pleasure painting the odd skirting board, door frame or window pane, as one would have had enjoying the beauty of the countryside or lying on a beach, without any feeling of resentment at being cheated out of, by some predetermined act of nature, that fateful suntan one has paid so dearly for.

By the end of January we'd had progress in the form of our first household bill written in euros, but the barn roof, which had been battened, had not otherwise progressed and was still at the mercy of the elements and the roofer. Tom and Annabel were managing to contain their frustrations and disguise their growing impatience well, by philosophically reminding themselves that the finished roof would look better than ever, and would put an end to their constant worries over the state of their roof generally. The work at *la grande maison blanche* had now finished and the house was back on the market, but attracting little interest. Only a handful of potential buyers required or could afford such a luxurious and expensive property offering a grand view of tree stumps occupying the area where the poplar plantation had once stood, and a distant view of the road. Perhaps we could contemplate a few more of the pleasant exchanges we used to enjoy before the owners eventually manage to sell the house. When our visits coincided there would occasionally be a knock at the kitchen door and an American voice would call out "Our water pressure is very poor. Is yours OK?" We would smile and shake our heads, quite resigned to the quirks of French country living. About fifteen minutes later an anxious face would appear at the door again. "We've now lost our water supply. Has your water supply gone, too?"

Once Audrey appeared at the door with a plateful of fresh fish they'd bought at the market that day, inquiring if we would like to have it, as they had decided to eat out that evening and they would not have a chance to enjoy it. Such acts of spontaneous generosity and thoughtfulness revealed much about the couple over and above their overall wealth. They would be greatly missed.

By the end of January the work on our own property had not yet begun. The assessment that had been due to take place in November had at last been completed and we were still awaiting the final costing, which seemed about right by the standards we had become accustomed to, and pretty well on target. We were living on tenterhooks, knowing we had left ourselves rather vulnerable by deliberately failing to empty the water taps in November, believing the workmen would be going into the house almost immediately. Fortunately there had been no winter frosts, unlike the weather we were experiencing in the UK, so in that respect all was well. Constant heavy rain over December and January had caused the tiny stream to swell and the area in proximity to the little bridge had flooded a couple of times. Kevin had decided to employ a tiler who would, hopefully, not manage to fill the dustbin full of broken tiles, effectively breaking every second tile – avoiding if at all possible, a dreaded third visit to the bricolage, to order yet more tiles. A visit to the Mairie was yet to be accomplished, but Kevin could envisage no problems there, as we would by all accounts, be enhancing windows that were already present, in elementary form at least. Work would begin on the *salle d'eau*, the garage ceiling and the two windows in mid-February, and should be finished all being well, by mid-March. On the home front at least, things were auspiciously moving according to plan.

Although these were perceived to be the last of the major tasks to be completed, we were not naive enough to believe that these would be the final ones, and that we could bask in the knowledge that from this time on we would be able to relax and just spend the rest of our lives enjoying the sun, the sand and the sights. Some friends of ours who had bought a shell of an old farmhouse in Provence, then were obliged to camp out in the garden for four years until it was fit to live in, named their house 'the money box' for good reason, even if it was a little tongue in cheek. There would always be new projects, new ideas, unforeseen expenses, paintwork to touch up every now and again; it was part of the excitement. The wall tiles in the kitchen could do with replacing, and tiles on the kitchen floor would look much smarter than the existing linoleum. It was a well-known fact that I was not too enamoured with the black and white floor tiles in the salon, which exhibited a rather cold appearance within the room. Soon the toilet window would need replacing; wood rot had been spotted in the wooden sill. There would be no end to the jobs, but that was all part of the fun when we visited the *gîte*.

Sometimes, beleaguered with icy winds, the snow and frosts of a typical English winter, we could just close our eyes and imagine we were sitting in the garden of our home in the Charente-Maritime, with the sun's warmth on our faces, looking over the sunflowers to where the dusky outline of the distant woods meets the vivid blue skies, or perhaps waving to the bunch of red-faced cyclists on their Sunday rally, puffing their way up the long steep slope of the lane.

We could actually smell the great conifer, with its giant cones that were capable of inflicting serious injury to anyone passing beneath, if a cone happened to fall at that precise moment. We would collect basketfuls of the giant cones every year. When they burned they produced a magnificent warm glow in the open fireplace. The tree was now so large its branches were impinging upon the passing telephone wires, something we would have to deal with before the authorities dealt with it in their own inimitable way.

The forsythia, the hibiscus, the sumach, the *lilas d'Inde*, even the privet hedge had each gained a third in height over the years in spite of frequent pruning. The white roses now completely covered the dry stone wall, punctuated by the occasional wild blackberry stems. We could sit in the shadow of the walnut tree and almost smell the apples on the tree behind and to the right of us, by the wall at the other side of the narrow grassy lane. The fragrant rosemary had grown to gigantic proportions, encouraged by its proximity to the outlet from the kitchen sink, which nestled close to its origins and poured its contents regularly on to the eagerly awaiting root mesh. In the border a delicate pink, sweet smelling rose thrust its way upwards each season into the cool shade between the branches of the sumach and was one of the most perfectly exquisite specimens we'd ever seen.

We could inhale the gently aromatic air, listen to the sounds of nature and watch until the sun's brilliant haze slowly faded into a mellow hue and dipped into obscurity beyond the horizon. It was in those brief moments, when our thoughts returned to our home in the French countryside, that our problems and anxieties appeared to dissolve and vanish with the disappearing sun, and there seemed no place on earth so enchanting or so inviting.

Keep up to date with the Léonie Press's latest books about France on our website: **www.leoniepress.com**

Just two of our books about the experiences of British people with French property

A BULL BY THE BACK DOOR

Written by ANNE LOADER
and illustrated by PATRICIA KELSALL

An unexpected legacy enables the Loader family to buy an old stone farmhouse in the depths of the French countryside. It has been unoccupied for years but they are drawn to the charm and dignity lying under the grime and cobwebs.

Even before the purchase goes through 'Les Anglais' are welcomed with genuine affection by their new neighbours. From their very first day at St Paradis they begin to make close and lasting friendships in spite of the language barriers.

But it is not only their neighbours who welcome them. Soon they are aware that the spirit of the former owner seems delighted to see her family home being restored to life. Indeed, it appears uncannily almost as if she has chosen the Loaders for this task.

ISBN 1 901253 06 6   Price: £8.99

LILAC AND ROSES

by PEGGY ANDERSON
edited by JAN BEVAN

The late Peggy and Alan Anderson bought La Clède, a ruined farmhouse near the appropriately named town of Joyeuse in the Ardèche, in 1963 – long before Peter Mayle appeared on the scene and made such purchases fashionable. Set amidst vineyards and sweet chestnuts, it cost £900 and they spent the next ten years, and most of their savings, renovating it. Their friends thought they were mad.

Yet by the time the couple came to retire they had transformed the ruin into an enchanting home. A local newspaper article described them as being set for "a life of lilac and roses". This delightful book was written in 1975 and has been edited by Peggy's daughter Jan Bevan as a tribute to her mother. It contains 18 b&w and colour photographs.

Jan now lets out half the house as a summer holiday *gîte* and lives in the other part.

ISBN 1901253 22 8   Price: £7.99